Become a Teacher

The Secrets to Become a Successful Teacher

(Advice for High School Students Who Want to Become Teachers)

Tracy Ramey

Published By **Darby Connor**

Tracy Ramey

All Rights Reserved

Become a Teacher: The Secrets to Become a Successful Teacher (Advice for High School Students Who Want to Become Teachers)

ISBN 978-1-77485-937-7

No part of this guidebook shall be reproduced in any form without permission in writing from the publisher except in the case of brief quotations embodied in critical articles or reviews.

Legal & Disclaimer

The information contained in this ebook is not designed to replace or take the place of any form of medicine or professional medical advice. The information in this ebook has been provided for educational & entertainment purposes only.

The information contained in this book has been compiled from sources deemed reliable, and it is accurate to the best of the Author's knowledge; however, the Author cannot guarantee its accuracy and validity and cannot be held liable for any errors or omissions. Changes are periodically made to this book. You must consult your doctor or get professional medical advice before using any of the suggested remedies, techniques, or information in this book.

Upon using the information contained in this book, you agree to hold harmless the Author from and against any damages, costs, and expenses, including any legal fees potentially resulting from the application of any of the information provided by this guide. This disclaimer applies to any damages or injury caused by the use and application, whether directly or indirectly, of any advice or information presented, whether for breach of contract, tort, negligence, personal injury, criminal intent, or under any other cause of action.

You agree to accept all risks of using the information presented inside this book. You need to consult a professional medical practitioner in order to ensure you are both able and healthy enough to participate in this program.

TABLE OF CONTENTS

Introduction 1

Chapter 1: The Good 2

Chapter 2: The Perks That Come In The Career 11

Chapter 3: The Bad 18

Chapter 4: In What Ways Do You Evaluate Teaching Prior To Making A Decision? ... 37

Chapter 5: Diamonds Of Teaching That Await You 45

Chapter 6: Offer An Excellent Learning Environment 112

Chapter 7: Planning And Management Learning Venues 135

Chapter 8: How To Work And Connect With Students 164

Conclusion 183

Introduction

This book has been specifically written for people looking to make to pursue a career in academic teaching. Be it school teacher or professor at a university, you will find essential information and guidance about how to begin your ideal career.

You may have your own reasons to become a Teacher or Lecturer, or following the paths that many successful individuals have already walked If you're truly interested in launching your own teaching career the classroom, this book will supply you with the necessary details and steps you'll need to start your journey.

The book is divided into two parts each with its specific set of information about how to become a teacher or Lecturer. There are many who progress from teaching to becoming Lecturers the book will prove helpful regardless of what your ideal job in teaching is. It also reveals that several of the suggestions contrast and compliment one another in both roles. They can serve as a complete set instructions and steps to follow to help anyone obtain the education and experience required to teach.

Chapter 1: The Good

Teachers make a significant influence upon the daily lives of students. This responsibility isn't a common feature of jobs, which makes it (for the appropriate person) an extremely rewarding career. Here are the top aspects of teaching:

Everyday is a brand new Experience

In the classroom the one thing you can be sure of will be that there won't ever be a day that will be identical. This isn't a typical office job that you carry out the same copy-and-paste chores or make the same phone calls every day the day at an insurance or recruiting company. As teaching, you're designing and preparing new lessons every day, and having to deal with various situations every day and the adjustments do not stop there. Each academic year , you'll be faced with the opportunity to teach a brand new class of students and a brand new team, a fresh class, new duties and possibly a raise If you're lucky. In other words, you'll never be bored in your job as teacher!

It's a rewarding experience

Teaching, in contrast to 95% of the jobs available is one that has a positive influence on our communities. Teachers witness massive growth among your students and the knowledge that you been a major part of the development of your pupils is an extremely satisfying experience. Let's face it, when you look around, who actually can claim that their job is a source of unquestionable importance that makes you feel that they're doing their part to make a difference in the world? Not many people. It is likely that for the majority of people their only joy they can get from their job will be at the conclusion of each month when their wages come through or they land an excellent bargain, both of which are purely personal satisfactions and are not a truer reflection of the world that reaches across a variety of futures and people.

Massive Impact on the Learning of Children

We all are aware that helping children learn things is enjoyable, fun to talk about, and has an important purpose; but did you think about the effect it has on an person? The impact that this individual has on them without having to show off or fuel your own self-esteem, is significant for their education. Through the guidance of their teacher, pupils learn to write and read, as well as analyze, experiment, test as well as observe and comprehend their surroundings. In a lesser way an experienced teacher can get pupils to jump up in their grades and be better on exams (both of which will lead the students to better futures). In a more modest yet perhaps more important scale twenty years from now, pupils could write using the method which you used to teach them; or calculating sums using the techniques that you taught them, employing the method you taught the students in PE; or teaching their students using the same passion the lessons you gave them. To sum up, please do not underestimate the importance that you play in children's education.

Massive Impact on Students' attitudes towards learning

Learning stuff is something but developing a positive relationship to learning is a completely different beast. Students may be aware of a wealth of relevant information and be capable of recalling a wealth of information however, if they don't like learning and don't enjoy the process, their chance of becoming a lifelong student is drastically decreased. As an educator, you play an indisputable role to play in fostering within every pupil the desire to learn. If you succeed in this massive job, students will leave the class with a new outlook about learning that can last for a lifetime. There are students who enter your classroom with an existing fear of learning and at the end of the year, they will have a genuine appreciation for the comprehension of various subjects and their newly acquired ability to communicate confidently. The best teachers create pupils who do not stop learning after school and continue to learn and eventually transfer it to the next generations. The teachers can help make education enjoyable as well as cool and last for a long time that have an enormous influence on the lives of their pupils.

Role Model

Excellent teachers provide their pupils with an ideal role model. You'll spend an extended period of time with your students, which means they'll undoubtedly learn certain values and habits you are a part of, including the good and the negative. If you lack of enthusiasm for learning then you can expect your students to show that in their own education. If you treat people with respect and compassion and respect, observe your students behave in this manner and if you value the process of learning, and are convinced about the purpose of learning observe how your students are also influenced by this belief. We are all five people that who we have the greatest time with So whether you whether you like it or not your students are likely to imitate the way you conduct yourself. This is a great chance for teachers to help shape students' values and opinions in a meaningful manner. I can still recall the way of my favorite PE teachers in school and how their experience and enthusiasm, paired with their humor and personality became my heroes as well as idols that I used to be a model for what I would like to do as a teacher.

We must not forget that, while certain children are blessed with positive role models however, others do not have any. A lot of children come from emotionally poor backgrounds, where they do not have a single person to admire to be a model. this is extremely sad, yet it's also extremely typical. In the case of some students, you'll be the sole consistent and positive person they have in their lives and the only one who can provide a reliable example from which they can learn invaluable life lessons. This is a massive responsibility yet is equally effective in its intent and an excellent reason to want to become a teacher in primary schools.

Support for Emotional Development

The students will most likely forget your words or lessons, but they will not forget how they felt. Children are going through a flurry of emotional growth all the way to adulthood. As an elementary school teacher, you'll play a role in observing and developing the emotional development of your students. It is a privilege to witness students gain confidence through the environment you have provided to allow them to develop. See children overcome challenges with confidence and overcome fears of failure, and engage in exciting activities since they desire to. In addition, watch their grit, cooperation and joy increase when you take charge of the classroom. You will also be a hand to them in their moments of struggle and need and struggle, you'll be there to help them, and you'll always be present to celebrate their accomplishments with sincerity.

Working with Children

Children are special, unique humorous, sincere innocent, joyful and curious (they have a variety of other things too but let's just be with these qualities at the moment!). Children are able to bring a smile to your face at a moment's notice smile, warm greetings, sincere praises and genuine delight in sharing their successes with you. In addition youngsters have an innocence that is so pure their lives, and the vast majority of them have no worries about life's pressures constraints, obligations and pressures. They live in the moment and can smile, cry and behave as if they are completely natural that can be truly delightful and something that lots of adults could be more of. Being able to work with children, for someone who loves children, is an enormous advantage to being an educator.

You can be creative

As an educator in a sense, you are the boss. This allows you to come up with new ideas for your classes and create them to be unique to the personality of your teacher (as as they follow the national curriculum, of course!). This freedom of thought is exemplified by the most skilled teachers, who right from the beginning in the school year are putting their zing of concepts to test, and developing their own ideas. If you're an artist and want to express yourself, the classroom of a primary school offers a chance to discover your creative side, whether that's creating captivating exhibits that fill the classroom, whatever they choose to use e.g. space, jungle, London, World War 2 or designing classes that are interesting as well as unique and thrilling e.g. hands-on science demonstrations, experiments, creating a large piece of artwork and incorporating a particular challenge or creating a dramatic of a specific subject. There are endless possibilities.

In addition to that, being creative is beneficial for your health. Even even if you don't consider yourself as a talented person, you'll surely be amazed by the concepts you'll develop if you spend the opportunity to spend a few weeks with similar-minded teachers. Let's face it, being creative isn't something you can get in all careers and a lot of jobs do not require that kind of creativity, which is what makes teaching a unique job.

Resource Galore

In the area of teaching planning assessment the behaviour of students, marking and classroom management, ideas for displaying as well as managing teachers, parents with challenging students as well as supporting learners with disabilities and everything else that has to be taught and learning, there's one thing you can be sure of that somebody has written or produced videos on the exact topic, offering the absolute best advice for those who are looking for the information. If you're looking for advice when you teach it is not a lonely job and there's a wealth of information available to help you make it easier. There are books on the market which have been written by instructors who've been at the highest level, These books are sold at very little money and contain the wisdom of teachers that are ten, twenty or thirty years older than you; invaluable guidance. A small investment in these books can provide you with plenty of suggestions of tips and tricks you could not have come across otherwise.

There's another resource available that is superior to other sources, and that is the internet. The internet is brimming with websites that provide valuable details on every aspect of teaching. Do you need a few ideas regarding managing your behaviour? Find videos. If you are in need of to find a PE team building exercise immediately you can use the search engine. Teaching isn't a specific field that just a handful of people have ever encountered, it's an immense profession that is home to millions of people worldwide and, fortunately for you, most of those million people don't keep their ideas and tips on their laptops or USB and communicate them to you on the internet. There's no reason to be alone.

Chapter 2: The Perks That Come In The Career
Finding a Job and Job Security
Teaching, in the present can be described as a career with an extremely favorable market for those looking to find a job. Up to 93% of the students who studied the Primary Education course at my university were able to get teaching positions within six months. The others realized that teaching wasn't the right choice suitable for them or decided that they'd be teaching supply initially. In essence, if you're granted Qualified Teacher Status after finishing your teacher education, you'll most likely be able to secure a job with a decent salary fairly quickly. Schools are in desperate need of teachers all over the country. there is a need for them. However, this doesn't mean every area is equal in their ease of obtaining the job. Certain areas can be difficult for employment if they are located near a teacher-training institution be sure to keep this in your mind.

Additionally that, when it comes to maintaining your job it is quite confident in your teaching career. Teachers are everywhere and, even if a school isn't able to extend your term, it will be right to switch schools. Be aware that schools within a particular area may be in constant communication which means there's the possibility of being blacklisted in an area when you're just going from school to school and doing something shocking.

Excellent Pay and Career Development Opportunities

Everyone has the notion that teachers earn little and that they are on the lowest of the pay scale however this could not be far from the truth depending on the kind of pay you're hoping to earn obviously! If you're going to get your degree and accept a teaching job at the 21st year, you'll be starting at just under PS22,000 a year and then a whopping PS27,000 for a year when you're teaching in London It isn't too awful to me. Additionally, if you're looking to be employed in London at a special education need school, you'll be starting with a minimum salary of PS30,000 per one year. This is impressive for the first year of a new career. In the event that you're about 21 or so I'm willing to wager that there will be only many people of who are your age and earning the same amount. In addition, the amount you earn will go up as well due to structure of the band for teachers which will result in an increase of PS1000 annually. This normal progression will go up to PS35,000 per year at which point you could be able to progress to the next step.

It's true that the increases in pay are accompanied by fantastic opportunities for career advancement. In just a few years, you could be aspiring to become an instructor, then after a few more, you could become a year group leader. Before you know it, you're in a top management team before you've been offered the position of head teacher. The entire process can be completed in 10 years or less if you're committed to your career and are determined but don't be fooled into thinking that the additional obligations don't cause additional stress. Whatever your choice, a career in teaching could easily get you into the PS50,000 per year range If you're adamant about it.

A lot of Holiday

You've heard of it and heard about it for a lengthy time. Teachers receive an amazing amount of holidays throughout the year, 13-15 weeks to be more specific. 13-15 weeks of annual leave is an incredible amount of time off when compared with the average of 20 to 28 days of holidays which is the norm in the vast majority of other professions. Whilst your friends and family are working practically every week of the year, looking forward to a select few dates in summer and Christmas, you can have the pleasure of not looking so far ahead, as you'll always have 2 weeks at Christmas and Easter, six weeks in the summer, and 3 weeks of half terms scattered throughout...amazing! Relax and have time to travel, without worrying how you've been. however, keep in mind that your travel may be a bit more expensive because of the peak time when your holiday is scheduled. Overall, holidays are an enormous advantage of teaching that should not be missed. You'll likely be more aware of this when you've worked previously in positions where you were limited to 20-28 days of holidays. If you're going the path of teaching straight from high school, college and university I'm sure you'll agree with me when I tell you the holidays you get are an indulgence.

Ability to work anywhere and from anyplace
Teachers are needed everywhere, in and everywhere. From the inner city London schools that are essentially the square slab of concrete as a playground or a village primary that is with greenery and valleys schools, and consequently teachers are all over the place. This puts you in an excellent job opportunity. There are many people who have work assignments for a particular firm, and therefore have to stay at their current location or risk being laid off or a cut in wages. For teachers, this isn't something you need to be concerned about. This gives you

the an opportunity to work and travel at various places across the country, regardless of whether you'd like to return to your home with your family, take in the bustle and excitement of the capital city, or even move to a new place all by yourself. It's always good to know that the area that you choose to live and work does not have to be permanent. If you choose to leave and your salary will not be affected, so enjoy your days ahead.

Opportunities to travel abroad

If you decide to become an educator, you'll provide a lot of opportunities to relocate and work in other countries. This is a rare opportunity particularly for jobs which aren't the highest paid, like teaching. There are a lot of British International Schools that are looking to recruit skilled teachers. Be aware that I mentioned experienced, as the majority of British International Schools worth going to will require at minimum two years of teaching experience which means there's no need to hop onto a plane just out of the university! Teaching opportunities at British International Schools are vast and may be found in amazing locations. Hong Kong, Singapore, Dubai, Qatar, Shanghai are just a few of the ones that are possible to mention. Additionally it is possible to teach in other schools in the world that do not follow the British curriculum. All over Europe, Brazil, Australia there are many opportunities to be taken advantage of. Volunteering through teaching is also a great chance to travel around the globe, and many teachers are able to help poor areas with expert instruction and education.

A Craft

Teaching, unlike many of other careers around the globe is a profession that requires a certain level of skill. It's something that you will need to keep working on in order to enhance your skills and grow more proficient. There will never come an exact moment when you've achieved mastery of teaching. Therefore, there is always something new to discover and incorporate into your routine. This makes teaching enjoyable and provides you with something to aim for. A great help to this, is of course the grades you earn as an educator, and of which the "outstanding" label is the ultimate goal. But even a great teacher has to adapt to the times to keep this status. A teacher who was outstanding in 2014 may not be the same as an exceptional teacher the year 2017. This is a clear indication of the speedy growth in the field of teaching, and how it is an evolving art form that has many layers to master. It is a stark contrast to the mundane jobs that have very little development and change throughout the years.

Flexibility for Kids

If you are a parent or are planning to have children while working employed as a teacher Your schedule and holidays are likely to coincide so that you're not paying excessive amount for nannies and vacation clubs. Your children will likely enjoy the same vacation time as you have, which means you will have a decent amount of time in the park, at the beach and visiting relatives, traveling across the globe and all of it. But, don't think that you will have greater time spent with your kids every year, compared to other positions such as teaching, since a job is not going to mean that you get more time with your children during the other months of the year. it is because you'll be busy during term .

Chapter 3: The Bad

The benefits of teaching are the most we learn about (or pay attention to) before deciding to pursue to pursue it as a career. A lot of people learn about the bad aspects but dismiss it as a distant background noise and ignore the importance of teaching; don't do this! This is the worst parts in the field, the ugly parts in the teaching profession and the things you need to be aware of before taking the final decision of whether or not to become a teacher.

Long, Long Hours and Heavy Workload

If you're thinking about an education career, there is a simple aspect you must be aware of teachers who work extremely long hours. It's commonplace that teachers at primary schools is expected to work more than 60 hours per week. I've had the pleasure of working many 70-hour weeks that's an incredible quantity of time spent each week. This could have negative effects on your wellbeing and health. There is no truth to the notion that teachers end their work when pupils go home around 3.10. Teachers may be observed for a long time into the night working through an interminable list of work to be finished in the following day, or else will be rearranged into a massive pile to be finished at an undetermined date. Teachers may start their day at 7 am and can stay there until the time of 8pm. it's not a job that follows the traditional 9-5 working schedule applies the same sway. This is a position that is incredibly long and intermittent.

Let me really detail the time I'd be working in a normal day (this is coming from someone who's probably slightly slower than average in completing tasks). To begin: 6.15am wake up, 6.50am leave, arrive at school around 7.25am and start doing physical preparation and other chores; 8.40am-3.15pm teach during the school daytime hours; 3.15 to 6-7pm marking books and planning lessons for the next day. 7.40pm until bedtime to finish anything you need to do. Then, when you throw in some staff meetings, at a minimum an hour of work on the weekend , and all of the other necessities like laundry, food or going to the bathroom and greeting your family when you arrive and leaving, you don't really have the time for any other thing. I've noticed that often when I'm free to be myself and do whatever it is I'm inspired to and then end up needing to do another thing or stay awake all night long, even after a reasonable time. Teachers often complain about the their lack of social interaction or complain that they wish there was more time for their personal lives. Don't be apathetic, they are stating the truth. Teaching can be a career which means that your personal life is an absence and is only given some glimpses of it in the holiday season. Furthermore, unlike the majority of jobs you work an established amount of time per week, in teaching , you simply have a job to complete and no matter how many hours you have to put in, those are your hours! The rules for working hours in the UK state that you should not be required to work for more than 48 hours per week, however this isn't true for teachers. Teachers can't simply say "I finished at 5 pm, so come back later" and work until the next day You must remain until the job is completed. In saying "stay" it's just to refer to the task at hand in the sense that most schools allow teachers to leave just after children are finished if they wish to (which obviously is a plus) however, they'll be required to finish their homework at home. Last but not least, I'll remind you that teachers' hours depend on a number of other variables, such as for instance, the number of books they are required to mark, and how precise they have to make them mark; their particular school in which they are a part as well as their size; the group they work with and how well they perform with their team; how thorough the lesson plan to be to effectively deliver them, etc. But there's one thing that is certain, and that is educators work long hours, which eventually take over some, of the evenings, if not all weekends. Please be aware of this before pursuing the teaching profession.

The holidays aren't always a free time.

While 13 to 15 weeks of holiday a year can be but you're not going to take all of these weeks without contemplating teaching. In the summer, you'll have to complete some classroom work before the beginning in the school year. at the very least, a week's worth of time will be necessary if you're brand new to the field and need to be prepared. In addition to the academic year work it's also possible to have some weeks of rest in which you'll try to complete your reports, make the planning, and also complete numerous other tasks that must be accomplished prior to the date of return. In general you can anticipate that at least some days off will be spent on work-related tasks.

High Expectations

Teachers are subjected to a great deal of pressure from different sources such as their school and the top management team; parents of pupils in their classes as well as the government or Ofsted. All of these forces come together to create an appropriate amount of expectations concerning what you can expect from your instruction. The school and its senior managers will have to pressure to achieve their goals in tests and grades. This expectation and stress will then be passed on to you and you will be expected to meet, in a few instances, totally unrealistic goals. Some teachers will supervise the teaching process closely and will constantly have their staff members asked to modify their practices. This is a bit gruelling after you've already taken the same path in certain things (weather it's tests or behaviour management, or even planning).

Parents have high expectations for their children, since you're taking care of their adorable angels. Parents will be keen to ensure they have a great teacher who is able to provide quality lessons This can be a challenge when you're a new teacher however, you will convince parents to accept you certainly.

The government is awash with expectations, and rules regulations, expectations and rules change constantly and are constantly changing. If you've seen a teacher talk about the subject, pay attention to the tone and you'll notice that it's usually not one that is happy! It's normal for politicians who have no experience in the classroom to completely alter the standards of education Teachers are often disorganized because of this, and the majority of the time it's the teachers who have to pay for these changes.

Finally, the expectations of Ofsted the notorious Ofsted. Ofsted are an organization that evaluates schools against a strict set of standards. They are able to place schools under special measures. They also are able to evaluate schools as being outstanding. However their standards are quite high. It can create a sense of anxiety when they phone to let you know that an inspection will take place next day, and it's quite a bit of pressure. In the end, it's a fact that one thing is that the same applies to schools and the senior management teams, parents as well as the government and Ofsted All of them expect only the top from you. This isn't a position in which there is no way to fail know that.

The Teacher Training Course is Intensive.

If you're looking to become a teacher it's not an easy process where only a little effort is required and in reality it's the ideal test to determine what you'll be doing as a full-time teacher. If you're on an PGCE or a three-year elementary education course it is a fact that one thing is for certain, the placement. Most of the time, you are not in control of the school in which you will be sent to, or the year group, for that matter depending on the institution you attend and the school you attend. You may not even be in the desired crucial stage. This could put you on a different path because schools differ greatly in the way they conduct their business. There are also the actual assignments that can differ in difficulty, but there is a common theme throughout the entire process, an abundance of papers.

During the teacher training process, there is a lot to do. Not only do you have to plan, evaluate marking, instruct and everything else but you must also create an incredible amount of paperwork which is generally completely and utterly pointless. The task can take many hours of time that can hinder your ability to design better teaching and concentrate on the most crucial aspect of teaching: teaching. It's going to be highly detailed lesson plans, which isn't required for a full-time teacher. you'll write individual and class observations following each lesson in the core; you'll write detailed evaluations of every lesson you teach; you'll have to write paragraphs every week about how you're in line with the standards of your teachers and being told to complete all it while marking 90 or more books per day as well as make plans (the correct method) lesson plans, prepare lessons, go to meetings and obviously, teach. To put it in perspective, at the end of every day at my midway place, I had to write up thorough evaluations of my main subject classes, which required me to write down the ways you could improve on your teaching, how I worked as well as the standards I had met, and how they relate in relation to national curricula. In addition, I had to make sure that my lessons were as thorough as they could be, and went over about two (sometimes three) full sides of A4 and I was required to write an extensive observation of two students for each lesson. Then I was required to mark the books as I completed an entire class assessment Then I had to write daily group observations every Friday, and record the evidence of me meeting the standards for the week (about one-third of an A4. The whole process is completed in conjunction with the usual duties of a teacher.

"But what is the reason you have to complete the paperwork?". The paper work must be completed since as a teacher in training you'll be observed and rated by a supervisor or an inspector. This is yet another reason why the degree of your position will vary greatly depending on the quality of that person who is watching, but do avoid thinking that your teacher is one of the most pleasant ones, as you can be sure that at the very least, for one of your assignments you'll be assessed by someone who's completely following the rules and has to look over every bit of useless documentation before deciding that it's not meeting the expectations. What you're doing in a teaching assignment is a matter of opinion, and what one judge believes is a failure however, another judge believes to be excellent; it's unfair, it's unfair, but that's exactly what it is. If you find yourself at the receiving end of a lot of criticism from an assessment Do not react defensively and just let them know that you're willing to improve and follow the advice they've advised you the next time they come to visit. not causing trouble for your assessment partner is the most unprofessional choice you could make since they hold all the power while there is hardly any. Be prepared to speak your mind but don't hesitate seek advice from them on a particular subject. They'll appreciate being the catalyst for your progress and will be less likely to dislike your work when it comes time to reviewing your time.

Another issue that could occur with teacher training programs is the environment you'll be assigned to and, more specifically, the teacher in the classroom that you'll be in. The relationship you have with the teacher is vital. A positive relationship probably result in the teacher standing to your side as well as giving you support whenever you need help as they understand that teaching is hard and would like you to cross the line. A negative relationship with this teacher could lead to an argument during class time, disputes, complaints or a lack of assistance and support , and a complete failure to support your needs if you are facing an assessment that is challenging or by the book. Of course, it is an element that can swing any way and, regardless it is something that you must know about. Try to be friendly with the teacher in your class in the best way you can!

If you add an extended commute to your teacher's place of work and then add everything else and you realize just how difficult the challenges of teacher training is. In most cases, as I mentioned earlier the school you attend will be selected by you, which means your commute may be a lengthy and difficult journey that is required to be completed at least twice per day. When I was in my three teacher education assignments I had the shortest commute of 50 minutes and my longest one was about an hour and a quarter. The location I worked in was London as well, and during the entire teacher education process I have some of my fondest memories involve sitting in the back of a bus , with my head against the window, and stuffing the contents of a Subway down my throat , because I knew that I would not have time to cook dinner once I arrived the next bus. Behind me was a gruelling day. before me was a sight of red light signals because of traffic, which was a nightmare. However, you could be in a location that is just a few minutes away from your front door, so be patient and hope for luck.

I'm not telling you this in order to make you feel like I'm trying to scare you. I'm just trying to get you to be aware that it's a complicated process, even when you're in the middle of things. You'll certainly be in shock when your teacher's assignments turn up the ante in terms of workload. But, on examination, I've never been more intensely in my life. So, although initially it felt like hell, today it's an accomplishment that I am proud of since I went beyond my limits and, from that point on, you'll know the meaning of hard work which is why other careers might seem like a bit of a slack when compared to. The teacher's training process is not easy as is being a teacher. is a tough job, but it's also quite different. So, just remember that both professions have the same angels and demons.

Pay isn't as high in relation to Hours

I've previously mentioned that the pay for teachers is fairly decent. I am still sticking to this view, but it is mostly based on a yearly basis. If you take it apart and look at the salary of teachers per year to the amount of hours they spend at their job, the pay of teachers is actually quite low. An example is that the average salary for an NQT is PS22,000 per year, while that's the lowest wage available for teachers in Great Britain is currently PS7.20. A NQT can expect to work for around 60 hours a week. If someone earning the minimum wage worked during those hours, they'd be making PS22,464 annually which is more than the NQT but holidays aren't included in the calculation. If you earned an amount that was a little more appealing of money, but not classified as a "big sum" for instance, PS10 for an hour. If working exactly the same hours as the typical primary school teacher and earning PS31,200 annually. PS31,200 is an excellent amountand it could have been earned with less pressure than the teacher's salary. If people say "don't join teaching to earn cash" They aren't in any way denying the reality of the amount, but also the amount of time it takes to to earn this amount. There are many 9-5 jobs available which pay 20, 30, 40 or more than 50 thousand pounds per year, most of them do not have the same rigors of a teaching profession. This is the reason if you are looking to earn money and think that teaching is the way to go it, you're mistaken. In the end, when it comes to it, how much will you put on your leisure time, your leisure time, and family time?

Teaching children is a huge responsibility

I've already mentioned that teachers can make tremendous influence in the lives of students This is certainly real. However when you consider that potential impact comes a significant amount of responsibility. It is your role as a child's model, the sole source of education , and for many, the most always positive person they know so you must to be a master at what you do! It's not a position where you just play around late on a Tuesday with nothing and then disappear into the furniture, and not be noticed by anyone. This is a job that affects the lives of people. It's a job that is serious and you have to consider it a serious job. If you do not take seriously the job, avoid becoming teacher. It's not good for you , or the kids.

It can be difficult to manage children. (Behaviour Management)

Okay, you know the importance of the planning, assessment and long hours, a the burden of work, difficult staff and parents, and all of it, but have you ever stood facing 30 kids with a lack of attention, and they are in need of you to fill in that gap or something else? Even with all the other duties dealing with children's behaviour, this is what teachers are often have found to be the most difficult part of their job. Since it is certain that throughout your teaching career, children will test and challenge your boundaries on every day and are likely to find weaknesses in your armor which they could use to take the power from your control and put it in their own hands. Because it is possible to ignore maths and English and maths, children are the most skilled in the degree to which a teacher's professionalism is as well as how high their likelihood of getting a sanction with certain adults. This is the reason you might enter a class that seems to be a perfect environment for children however, if you replace that teacher with a shaky and less secure teacher, and the children could be climbing up the walls and creating chaos that you have never experienced before in just 30 minutes. The management of children's behavior isn't easy and, even more so it could take some time to truly understand how to manage your classroom. Poor behavior can make the classroom frustrating, slow, and repetitive and leave you wondering what the point all. You won't understand this until you've got thirty students causing disarray in your class shouting, running around about stories, telling stories, and throwing things, and you're the person responsible for in charge of their behavior. Unruly behavior can really dampen the enjoyment of teaching because it could become an obstacle to great lessons. In addition, poor behavior could have a major impact on stress levels. When I was a child I can remember children screaming after I had taught an unsatisfactory lesson in the afternoon following wet play. Children were throwing, fighting at each other, shouting, and, in general totally out of control! However much I yelled or tried to control the situation, I could not, even if the teacher, or someone else had come into the classroom, I could be thrown out on the spot, provided I didn't fall over in embarrassment in the first place. I remember standing there , in silence for some time, gazing towards my fingers to determine whether they were there, and to determine if this was happening, and sure it was. However, you need to realize that behavior management takes time and, if you work to improve it regularly, you'll surely improve and eventually are in a class with perfect angels who desire absolutely nothing else than give total attention throughout your classes.

Underestimating Pupils' Complexity

Children are extremely complicated and have a wide variety of requirements. As a teacher, you have to be aware of the needs of your students and adjust your curriculum to ensure that all students are involved and achieving at the same levels. Be aware that this could be a challenge given the wide range of abilities within your class: some students have a talent or gift that is unique which means you'll need develop additional ways to encourage them. the majority of students will fall between the middle and your "core" group and finally, some of the children in your class will be poor achievers who find the work they do too difficult, so you should provide them with classes that are equally accessible and accessible. You can do this by assigning them various goals, criteria for success and resources or assigning an TA to help the students. When you're creating fantastic lessons, one size will not suit all. You have to consider the various abilities and make sure that everyone is involved.

If I tell you to ensure sure that everyone is inclusive, that also includes pupils with special educational needs (SEN) as well as pupils who speak English as an additional Language (EAL). They will most likely be in your classes, but they are not always supported by a 1:1 ratio to 1 support program and it is likely that they will not. When it comes to SEN, about 15% of students in England are SEN and that's only those with an official statement. This means that in your classroom , you will have three or more students with SEN. The term "SEN" can take on diverse forms, including autism, dyspraxia; down syndrome the social and emotional issues as well as speech, language and communication needs, and so on. As a teacher in the classroom you'll require an extensive understanding of these students and a thorough knowledge of how to incorporate them into your classes.

English in addition to other languages is something which some of your students might be able to speak, for instance in London or other ethnically diverse regions of the country. The majority of your class might have English as an alternative language. It is also necessary to plan your lessons to ensure that these students are included. This isn't an easy task, but not impossible!

Needs a lot of energy (Physically draining)

Teaching can be a physically exhausting job. No matter what you did on the weekend, or how late you got to sleep, or how much work you've put in since the children went home yesterday afternoon You still need to be that enthusiastic and happy teacher in when they arrive in the morning and continue to maintain that enthusiasm throughout the day. If you fail to maintain that enthusiasm, your students will notice, and your attitude and willingness to study will be a reflection of on your inability to get going. This is the reason why many teachers say that teaching is an acting job , and they have to be in character. If your behavior is off, the kids are likely to pick it up and respect will be lost. Because of this, teaching can be a very mentally demanding job. Not to mention it is a constant reminder to instructing kids to stop doing small things.

Schools vary greatly

I've previously mentioned this in others, however it is an array of schools. A fantastic teacher could be a victim at a school that is not a good one and a mediocre teacher may appear to be a top teacher at a prestigious school. The school you attend is what matters! The right school for you can significantly reduce the workload. What questions you should ask are: Will you be organizing in a team? Are you using just one form entry or multiple entries? How much marking is required to mark? How precise must your marking be? How many NQT's are there in the school? What is the time when teachers are departing? Are teachers satisfied?

Are there high levels of staff turnover? Did you check out the most recent Ofsted report? Schools differ in every one of these areas. If you're planning to be selective, you might look at the location and area of the school as well as the level of staff's experience. The most important thing to remember, is that there are no two schools that are identical, so don't think that your new school will have the same workload or stress levels as the previous one!

Chapter 4: In What Ways Do You Evaluate

Teaching Prior To Making A Decision?

If you take one thing out of this book, it should be the following...

It is essential to test your teaching skills before you decide whether or not to do it in a career!

You must be tested for teaching skills and gain plenty of classroom experience prior to you begin your journey into teaching The more experience you have, the more valuable. It is because a lot of individuals decide to teach without knowing the requirements for profession. I've tried to highlight as much as I can, however you will not fully know what it's like to work in a classroom until you've been within one, in actual. Below, I've listed some helpful tips to help you test your teaching.

1. Participate in a class. The course you're applying for may have you spending time in the classroom prior to joining whatever amount of time they want volunteers for and then double it. My college required me to spend 10 days of classroom work but this isn't enough time to be able to make an informed decision about the possibility of becoming an educator. I would recommend spending two months in the classroom over the course of one summer. You

should also be able to go to the classroom once per week to spend an afternoon during the year. The time in blocks will let you observe the teacher and classroom for one full week. It will help you understand students a bit more clearly, and reveal what life in the classroom really feels like (not what you think it's like).

2. You should be working in a school, preferably. It's true that this isn't be a viable option for all however, working at the school system is a good opportunity to see the way they operate and determine whether teaching could be the right match for you. If you're unsure and have a amount to be flexible in the current position look into a job at the school system, it might be the perfect fit for you or maybe not.

3. Shadow an instructor. This goes hand in with volunteering, but instead of going in and out with the children, you should inquire with a teacher if could shadow them for the entire day. This allows you to witness the whole process in teaching and not only the teaching aspect. Watch their preparation during the day, how they mark following school, and their plans This may be boring for you, but it is an excellent way to understand the subject matter you're learning about.

4. Take time to visit various schools. This is another important step to take before making the plunge. Being a volunteer for all of your time at one school and only one class is like visiting an ice-cream shop choosing vanilla, and then believing you've tasted all the flavors of ice-cream due to it...you don't. The primary school you attend could be chaotic and chaotic with a lot of kids who don't know how to follow the rules of order. However, if you only go to one school only to decide it's not suitable for you, then you've missed out on the chance to visit different schools that aren't like the one you've been to, schools that are calm and relaxing environments to be. The reverse is also true when you just visit one school and that one is peaceful, beautiful and the kids are well behaved, you should visit a classroom or a school in which that's not an issue, which will give you an overall perspective of what classrooms could be.

5. Do a bit of teaching. If you have the chance while volunteering (an possibility you'll need to request) take the opportunity to try a bit of teaching. The more you can do, the more. It doesn't matter if you lead a group of six students for a 20-minute lesson, or give a subject-based class during the day (art or geography, PE, history) Both will provide you a

great understanding of the process of teaching and what it's experience is like at the time it is a moment that's difficult to capture while you're reading an article or watching a movie. This is something I'd recommend you to pursue in your volunteer work at schools.

6. Talk and walk. In the school you volunteer in, take a stroll around the school and take in the atmosphere Take a look around at the displays as you watch the kids play in the play area, and watch the teachers instruct and think about the question: do I feel at home within this particular environment? Equally, talk. Talk to your teachers, speak with other staff members Talk to NQTs, talk to teachers and more importantly, talk with the children. Consider the following questions: do I get along well with children? Do I enjoy children? Can I be a part of a team all day long with children?

In addition make sure you talk to your loved ones and friends about your decision, since it could affect them as well as they could have some helpful tips to share. If you're really dedicated then you'll have to cut off your social networks and meet with people who are in training as teachers or who are teachers, or are in the same situation like you.

Ultimately, GET SOME EXPERIENCE BEFORE DECIDING TO TEACH!! !

Are You Doing It For the right or wrong reasons?

Once you've considered all factors of teaching you need to be honest about whether you're joining this profession for the right or incorrect motives. For this portion of this book to get the best possible outcome it is essential to be transparent about your own feelings when it comes to your choices. This is where I will list the best motives, the reasons that are not so good and the arguments that are completely irrelevant to the choice you make. As you read write down your reasons, and then decide which category they belong in.

Good Motives

* You enjoy having children around in an a classroom and would like to continue doing this. (Really think about this question, do you like working with children? What are you able to tell? Have you had any knowledge of an educational environment?)

* You want to be a an example of positive behavior to youngsters.

You're passionate about learning and are convinced of the positive impact it has on the lives of people's lives.

* You're looking forward to being an integral part of the emotional development.

You are a lover for discovering new things and you want to encourage youngsters to see learning the same way as you.

Bad Causes

Children are just so adorable. because they're adorable and you want to cuddle them. (Teaching isn't like this.)

* You're looking to be creative on your work. (This argument isn't an adequate reason by itself).

* As school days are brief, you'll be able to go off at half-past three each afternoon.

* You're looking for work which is a craft, and that you are able to develop. (Like the point about creativity it is a valid argument in some instances however, on its own it's an unsound reason since there are plenty of jobs that require skills to be developed and learned).

Reasons that are not relevant

I recommend that these factors aren't even taken into consideration when making your decisions. This is due to the fact that these factors should be thought of as bonus points If you love having children around and have checked a few important boxes. If you've not highlighted any of the above reasons which resonate with you or you're not sure, go for the opportunity to learn more or, more importantly consider rethinking your career. These reasons

are totally irrelevant to the decision you are making
* Lots of gifts for the holidays
Good opportunity to earn a good salary and advance in your career
* Flexibility for children
* Good pension
* Possibility to work in a foreign country
* Security of employment
* Opportunities to work anywhere and everywhere in the world.

If you've thought about it in depth to experience classrooms, but these unimportant motives are your sole reason for choosing a profession with teaching please do yourself a huge favor and do not become a teacher. These are fantastic perks however, it is an obsession with work therefore you should not consider it a career just for the perks. Be a teacher because would like to teach and you'd like to be around children. If you're looking to work in a classroom and teach children is one of the reasons to consider joining teaching, then you'll get a license to enjoy the benefits and advantages of teaching. But, if the desire to teach children in an educational environment isn't at the top of your list of motives, then it's probably time to rethink your decision (or at least learn more about the classroom) as teaching can be a difficult task when you don't have the desire to do it with passion.

Chapter 5: Diamonds Of Teaching That Await You

In this course, we'll be studying the 7 Facets of Teaching as well as the 35 elements of Instructional Intervention which empower these.

This experience will allow you to build two key competencies Both of which are vital to top-quality teaching. The first is your understanding of the various aspects which contribute to better education and training. Second is the ability to apply this information effectively when working with students.

As time goes on as we go, you will be guided gradually to identify, understand the superior skills. The more you use these skills, the better you'll be able to instruct and the more your students will gain. It's that easy.

While reading this, please be conscious that this Guidebook is a guidebook with one main objective, and that is to help you to teach in a way that fosters a positive, enjoyable learning experience for your students.

With that in mind, let's start our journey through the seven Facets that make up Superior Instruction. in highlighting their potential and strengths and their effectiveness. We will also discuss the training they require to be implemented, the method of implementation and the ways they help both you and the students collaborate in harmony. Keep in mind that every Facet contains a selected set of extremely effective methods and conditions for teachers. Make sure you are able to comprehend and apply them efficiently.

Let's move on through Facet 1.

Facet 1 - Project an Outstanding Teaching Personality

Your goal is to develop and demonstrate a persona of teaching that students will find interesting accessible, helpful skilled, knowledgeable with a balanced, positive and inspiring.

Concerning the Quality of Personas

You've seen that your teaching personality is your personality when you interact with students. When you are at your best it is a Persona has a variety of appealing, useful traits that help you in your teaching skills and encourage your students to cooperate.

It's important to recognize that your professional image will differ somewhat from your typical persona, but it's little concern. Ask yourself "If I were an in-class student What would I expect of my instructor? What would I prefer to feel treated? What do I like the most? What do I want to discover? What could I do to enjoy doing it? What kind of learning environments will be most beneficial for me, day in and every day?" Your answers then provide suggestions on how you can perform your best.

However, students, particularly those in the younger years don't think in these terms. So, you have to answer the questions you have for yourself, and taking into consideration that the most effective teachers accomplish two things simultaneously to show their proficiency as instructors. They first infuse their teaching with tasks and conditions that students) love and 2)) are interested in learning. While there are instances, the combination of teacher efficacy and students' enjoyment is the key to a successful teaching. Keep that in your mind.

Let's get started Start by examining the curriculum guidelines for your school that states your students must be taught. If the suggested learning activities aren't appealing enough to students, try adding sparks with stories or contests, questions or projects, learning games pantomimes and the similar. You can also include something that students are particularly interested in learning. When you do that you'll see that students' cooperation increases as does learning speed and the outcomes persist for a long time.

Keep this in mind It is your professional obligation to engage with your students in ways that show the qualities of kindness, charisma compassion, understanding determination, perseverance, and an unending determination to assist. If you refine those skills and demonstrate them consistently it is certain that you will have an influence to your student's experience, particularly in their relationship with you and how much they are learning and how they remember.

With these in mind Let's take a moment to consider some of the observations made by revered experts in the field of teaching and learning. These ideas even though they aren't yet tested in research they will most likely improve your teaching and strengthen the relationships you have with your students and the parents and guardians of their children.

James P. Comer on the importance of the relationship between students and teachers

James P. Comer (2015) is a professor of child Psychiatry who, for a long time, worked with schools located in low-income regions, concluded that no important learning happens in schools when teachers do not establish strong bonds to their pupils. In 1968, he established his School Development Program that helped teachers establish bonds with students as a method to improve the students' comfort, confidence and ability. Since its inception Comer's program was used in more than 1,000 schools. Enter 'James P. Comer, 2015. Remember to connect with your students.

Dale Carnegie on How to Influence Others

While Dale Carnegie (1936) did not directly address teachers, we can certainly benefit from his ideas that he offered in a fascinating manner. His advice is just as pertinent in the present as it was when it first was published.

If you'd like to, check with the local bookshops to see whether they have copies of his guidebook How to Win Friends and influence People. For a quick alternative, get a brief outline of Carnegie's advice by entering into an Internet browser the phrase 'Dale Carnegie 1936. Then, search for "The Best Summary of How to win Friends and influence People," which is an extremely brief summary of Carnegie's instructions about how to interact with people (in the case of students and their guardians or parents as well as our teacher colleagues) and get them to be drawn to us, convince them to our way to think, and eventually alter their opinions without creating anger (indeed an asset).

Carnegie's suggestions are highly valuable. If you come across this synopsis, make sure you save it in your pocket for reference and keep practicing the suggestions. One source, if you absorb and implement its ideas will improve your performance not just in working with students but with their families as well as your colleagues and friends and everyone else from every aspect of your life. It is truly a treasure. Keep in mind its primary quality: Positivity, Friendliness and consideration.

Effective Mind Control with The Power of Optimism

The Effective mind Control (accessed in the year 2019) is an online resource that encourages teachers to promote confidence in their students while minimizing negative impact of negativity. It gives specific tips for building a classroom positive attitude that enhances students' learning, enthusiasm and willingness to tackle the challenges.

To visit this website you must type into your browser "effective brain control'. You will discover three essential facts for teachers everywhere: first the fact that both optimism and pessimism are learned patterns in behaviour; second, that optimism is based on anticipations of capability and pleasure as well as optimism is based on fears of difficulties or unpleasantness. These concepts can be understood by themselves, are simple to implement and simple for students to comprehend. Remember: Optimism yes, Pessimism no.

William Glasser on Believing in Students

William Glasser (2001), one of the most influential educational advisors and commentators who urged teachers to believe that everyone are capable of achieving their goals in school. To demonstrate that they can succeed, he advised teachers to employ persuasive influence instead of coercion when they interact with students. The most effective methods of influence include engaging with students, showing respect, encouraging them and asking them for their opinion as well as suggesting alternatives and demonstrating your trust in your students. Make sure to show that you Have Faith in Your Students and Trust Your Students.

Marvin Marshall on The Downside of Coercion

Marvin Marshall (2016), as did William Glasser, has concluded that students don't learn well when forced to learn, however they can learn effectively when given the opportunity to make their own choices regarding what and how they would like to learn - within reasonable limits and of course. Marshall is also of the opinion that when students are given the opportunity to make their own choices and make their own choices, they develop an awareness of their own capacity and capability to make informed choices on their own. When they make these choices they are able to become more aware and behave correctly.

Marshall and Glasser have also stressed that to connect positively with your students and encourage them to realize the advantages that come from respect and civility. In order to do this by providing examples, encourage them to practice what these examples demonstrate and express your gratitude when your students demonstrate these traits at school.

In the end, think about these things: incorporate positive energy and civility in all interactions with your students. Show a warm and attentive manner, learn quickly and remember names of students Also, you should always acknowledge every student in turn, talk with them what they enjoy the most about school and with teachers, and be attentive to any concerns they may have. Keep in mind: trust, optimism and optimism.

More on the process of developing and displaying the Quality Teacher Personality

We've noticed that your personality as a teacher is the professional image you exhibit when working with students. And we've seen that it's an enhanced version of your persona, with a touch of charisma, interaction with students, consideration for their requirements, and a collection of effective and enjoyable techniques and methods of teaching. Below are some additional suggestions that you can use.

When you first meet with students, communicate to them the goals of learning for the class. State them not as a set of requirements, but rather as potentials, aspirations and beneficial results. Discuss your general style of teaching (organized engaging, stimulating, attractive fun, and beneficial by asking questions and suggestions instead of lecturing and judging). Explain how you plan to utilize instructional strategies that students will find beneficial and enjoyable including reciprocal learning and the concept of change. These will be further explained in this guidebook.

Also, explain how you intend to create an atmosphere in the classroom that is positive as well as a feeling of helpfulness and satisfaction as well as how you plan to employ guidance and feedback to ensure that everyone is focused, learning, and moving forward. This will allow you to build respect and trust with your students.

A note of caution: Although an effective persona for teaching is relatively simple to establish, it's nevertheless fragile. It is sometimes destroyed by just a word or facial expression. Therefore, make sure to remove from your interaction style any indications of arrogance, sarcasm and snide remarks or negative critiques, as well as jokes or remarks that may be offensive to others. A lot of times, those elements are detrimental to your success. Also, you lose credibility if you don't explain or clarify what you expect students to understand. Also, if you display your lack of concern for the students' needs. Or make unreasonable demands. or teach in an unorganized method. You may not keep your word on what you have promised.

Summary: Four Gems of Facet One. Your High-Quality Persona

Be sure to include the following "jewels of teaching in your Teacher Persona. They will benefit you and your students effectively. Consider them as traits found in the top teachers.

Your apparent knowledge and enthusiasm working with students

The constant emphasis you place on the importance of fairness, optimism and your constant efforts
• Your faith in the potential and goodness of all students
• Clarity, consideration and competence in all you say and do.

END OF FACET 1 INPUT - PLEASE PROCEED TO PRACTICUM 1

Practice 1 - Projecting the Quality of a Teaching Persona

Reminders

As stated as noted, the seven instructional aspects in this guidebook are divided into two sections. The first provides factual details and tips for growing your knowledge of various teaching techniques. We've completed that portion of Facet 1. The second component of each Facet--the Practicum , where we are currently can help you develop strong knowledge of teaching and other aspects of teaching students. Complete the exercises below with diligence.

But first, look for and find Collaboration This is a must! !

To get the most benefit You are strongly urged to form a study group with at least one other students to discuss and participate in the concepts that are presented in every Practical. An study team of 3 is the ideal. Even just one person is superior to working on your own.

Warm-up Quiz

Take a look at the following test. The correct answers will not be provided.

1. A Teaching Personality is A) one's personality that is naturally innate as well as the same for all teachers,) the same for all teachers c) the teaching personality of the person, and d) being able to be standardized quickly

2. The longest-running most-respected authority on interfacing with others:) Carnegie, b) Marshall, Comer,) Comer, D) The Power of Mind Control

3. Which of the following tones are most effective in encouraging learning?) peace,) laughter,) cute sarcasm) optimism

4. "How do I respond to, act, or express the above in a constructive and positive way"? is a reflection of the following sources:) Dewey, b) Comer, C) Glasser, d) Effective Mind Control

5. Who in 1968, developed a program to assist teachers create solid bonds with their students The program was: 1.) Glasser, b) Piaget, C) Comer, D) effective Mind Control

6. Which of these characteristics is the most effective for promoting learning? a) Charisma,

b) native intelligence,) high IQ or the common touch,) using the standard touch

7. "A gentle manner of kindness and understanding" A phrase that is described in this context as "a) misleading or misleading, (b) desired and in c) difficult,) suspicious

8. Your Author's assessment of the strength of the teacher's persona as follows: a) weak (b) moderate,) moderate strong, moderate,) strong and D) unclear

9. According to Glasser beliefs of teachers among students is one of the following: the following:) most important and a) not tested and (c) suspicious or indisputably important, and) moderately significant

10. Your Author's assessment of the impact of teacher personality on learning A) solidly reliable,) fragile and inconsequential,) insignificant for students who are motivated and d) not reliable

Terms and Concepts of the Core Concepts and Terminology

Discuss the nature of the topics listed below and discuss their likely impacts on learning: the persona of the teacher The Carnegie contentions, positive optimistic, students' choice trust in teachers and teachers, coercion by teachers, trust between the teacher and students.

Your Graphic Illustration of the Persona Teaching

On a single piece of paper, create a conceptual map of the teaching Persona along with its constituents and their effects as explained in the following. Create a presentation that is appealing, memorable, and simple to follow. (To discover a variety of styles, type the word "concept mapping" in the search bar of your Internet web browser.)

Make Practice using Your Concept Map

Create a concept map that you can use to describe using your own language the purpose and significance of the conclusions that you've made out of Facet 1. Make sure you are clear and have a logic. Learn with other learners and save this concept map as well as your other ones to come, to further review and reference.

Your personal 7-Point Summary of Facet 1

Determine the seven most significant concepts or ideas that you came across during this aspect of Teaching. Based on your knowledge, you can do these three actions:

1. Put the ideas or concepts in order of their effect you believe they will influence learning
2. Be able to communicate the concepts of the 7 in your own words and
3. Discuss and compare your work and conclusions with your fellow learners.

Start forming your ideal teaching Persona

1. Identify and describe the purpose of the teaching persona.

5. List the five characteristics of teachers you think will benefit students the most.

Practice with a Partner

With a teacher or before an mirror, you can present two actions you could demonstrate to students that you are keeping their best interests at heart. Tips: demonstrate sincerity, clarity and humor and facial expressions. Also, show body posture, gestures and even acting.

END OF FACET 1 - PLEASE PROCEED TO FACET 2

Facet 2 - You Display Control of the subjects you teach

Your objective is to learn and demonstrate a strong grasp of the subject that you instruct, your syllabus you will follow as well as the lessons you'll teach.

Terms and Concepts of the Core Concepts and Terminology

This Facet by examining the significance of curriculum, subject matter, lessons, objectives and other related issues in teaching:

Subject matter is the collection of information, rules and procedures. which you have to assist students in learning. You must be knowledgeable about these elements particularly their characteristics the values, their applications, and.

Curriculum is the broad program for learning by students that outlines first the subjects, facts principles, procedures, and topics your students must be taught (the subjects) as well as when, what, how and in what conditions you will be able to best impart the subject for your pupils, make sure that they are learning, and evaluate their performance. The majority of these issues are laid out in the curriculum guide that is provided to you by the institution in which you teach. You must follow the guidelines carefully.

Lessons are organized presentation and activities you give to aid students in acquiring abilities and knowledge. They also aid them in remembering the information they have learned and be competent in applying it.

The Learning Objectives refer to the precise outcomes (knowledge and competencies, etc.) that your students will be required to reach in the lessons you teach. The outcomes you expect your students to achieve are usually stated by observing student behavior (what students are saying and doing which you can be able to observe). Students will, for instance, be proficient in multiplying negative numbers, and describe the process for doing the same.

The Methods of Instruction refer to formalized methods you employ to teach students. They are not subjects themselves they are methods to organize and present the information for easier and better understanding. The most effective methods for instruction include Direct Instruction, Problem Solving and Class Discussion and Reciprocal Instruction. They are extensively used and have been found to be effective.

Strategies for Instruction refers to plans you create to engage students and assisting them to learn more efficiently. Examples of these are engaging challenges, real-world problem-solving group competitions, debates as well as experiments. You can also have students perform the ideas.

The procedures of instruction are sequences of steps you use to aid students in reaching the objectives stated. The term "procedures" can be interpreted as a steps that result in the fulfillment of the objectives for example, steps in working through problems, actions for finishing assignments, and the steps to write essays and paragraphs.

"The Big Picture in Teaching refers to the broad-based outline of all that the students should expect to know about specific subjects and subject areas. To fit into that overall view, lessons are planned and taught to aid students in understanding the many components that are incorporated into that larger picture.

Research supports proves that teachers with a strong grasp of the subject matter as well as curriculum and instructional techniques actually encourage students' learning to the extent that is above the average. To illustrate there are three research papers that confirm this assertion. If you'd like they were available, you can read them as well as other research reports via the Internet:

• Metzler, J., and Woessmann, L. (2010) discovered a positive correlation between teacher's knowledge levels of the subject and the students' resulting learning. To view this report, simply type in your browser "Metzler, J. and Woessmann, L. 2010

• Sadler, P., Sonnert, G., Coyle, H., Cook-Smith, N., and Miller, J. (2013) discovered strong connections between teacher knowledge and education of students in Middle School classes in physical science. The study is Internet accessible through 'sadler and al. sage 2013.'

* Ball, D., and McDiarmid, G. (1990) gave a thorough discussion of the role of subject matter in the teaching. The topic is called "Subject Matter preparation of Teachers and

can be Internet accessible. Browser"Ball and MacDiarmid, 90 subject matter.'

Ball and MacDiarmid claim they are of the aims of education is to allow students to engage in, not just learn about the major fields of human inquiry and thought like the past and how it relates to the present, our natural environment; concepts beliefs, values, and convictions that are shared by different populations as well as the dimension of space as well as the quantity aesthetics and the way they are represented as well as many more. These authors study emphasize that for students to be fully engaged in these areas of study they should be taught how to recognize, investigate and find practical solutions to real-world problems.

The "Big Picture" emphasis in the subject Matter

It is well-known, and is emphasized throughout the Guidebook that students can learn more and faster when teachers start lessons or a sequences of lessons by providing an introduction to the "big picture' of what needs to be taught. This means providing the subject with a captivating manner by describing its importance as well as highlighting its key content, and demonstrating the best way to learn those topics. learnt. Below are some of the Internet content you may want to read for further information on big picture instructional strategies:

>> Classroom Compass (September 2002) included three interesting pieces that examined the importance of 'big picture' in science and mathematics and science, as well as a discussion of the challenges that teachers often face and the ways that those issues could be resolved. These articles are informative and worth reading for teachers of all levels. To read the article simply type in your browser the phrase 'Getting to root of (subject) issue'.

The authors Josh Edwards and Joanne Edwards (2013) They provide a thorough explanation of the big picture approach to teaching along with the best practices for using it. To read their article "Getting the Big Idea Concept-Based Learning and Teaching In your browser the phrase 'big idea in teaching and learning. It will show you a variety of useful writings.

The author, Kevin Parr (2014) presents illustrations of teachers who use big-picture techniques and students in contrast to detail-focused students and teachers as well as provides guidelines for moving toward the use of big picture approaches. Read his article on 'Big-Picture Thinking and Detail-focused thinkers Impacts on Teachers and Students. It is accessible via "Parr. Big-Picture Thinkers.'

Subject Curriculum and Matter Teaching: What to Teach When, when, and How

We have observed that 'subject matter' is the set of knowledge, understandings, and abilities that students must acquire. We also have observed that research has proven that the more extensive teachers' understanding of the topics they instruct, the better their students are taught.

For 'curriculum', we've seen that it's a manual which outlines what you're to be teaching, when and how to impart it. In general the more you adhere to the prescribed curriculum as well, the better your students will do in achievement tests.

In the past, textbook authors offered instruction guides that teachers could follow. The guides, typically included inside the Teacher's Edition with suggestions for topics to be focused on, a central concepts, crucial methods, exercises to learn methods of assessing student performance, and in certain instances, test items for teachers to utilize. A lot of teachers utilized these guides, but many didn't.

The curricula of the majority of schools are designed by teams of teachers and experts, or are developed from existing frameworks used in other countries. In both instances schools select books that meet, enhance the curriculum, and provide explanations for it. Schools generally post their curriculum on the Internet for parents to view and other individuals. For examples, you may want to look up the California State Curriculum, which is accessible via the Internet. It's a lot of information. If you'd prefer to see an easier-to-understand presentation you can type into your browser "California Fifth Grade Literacy Curriculum. Once the site loads you can scroll to page 5.9 to find out more details.

For a more succinct overview of a school's complete 5th Grade program, clearly laid out all on one sheet, click here to check out the one from Doyle Elementary School located in San Diego, California. The site is directed to parents and guardians this Doyle program is concisely laid out but is also very instructive. To get it, type in your web Internet browser "Doyle Elementary Fifth Grade Curriculum."

Every school strives to make sure that their curriculums cover the subjects covered by the standardized tests which are later used to evaluate the progress of students. The results of these tests are a significant factor in measuring the effectiveness of the teachers and schools. As you can imagine, teachers and school staff take these tests extremely carefully.

Further information on effective teaching

For more information on the qualities that make highly effective teachers make sure you go through the following Internet content which are concise and informative;

> Killian, S. (2017). What makes a great teacher? The 7 Principal Attributes. Type into your browser: 'S. Killian 2017 is a great instructor.' Killian says there's no doubt that teachers significantly impact in the way students perform at school, however for a variety of reasons it's not always the case for all teachers to are able to do this, which indicates that certain teachers are better at delivering instruction than others.

Killian provides evidence from Barber, M. and Mourshed, M. (2007) who claim that students who are placed in schools with better-performing teachers typically learn three times as quickly as students with teachers who are less effective.

What are the distinctions between teachers who perform well and those who aren't? Barber and Mourshed claim that teachers who are highly effective have five characteristics that distinguish them:

1. They show a love for teaching.

2. They possess personal characteristics that entice students.
3. They are experts in the field they are teaching.
4. They use more effective methods of teaching.
5. They have higher expectations for their students

Killian's Internet article, that is worth your time, provides seven qualities of a teacher which contribute to excellent levels of student learning.

The author Meer, S. (2016) published an Internet article titled 7 Qualities and Characteristics of a Great Teacher. Browser: 'Meer, S. 2016 Top 7 characteristics.'

Meer says that every teacher wants to be successful in their jobs, yet many do not because they are not well-informed about the skills and knowledge that are the foundation of excellent teaching.

Meer Then, he lays out his list of top teaching competencies. Check out what he writes about the impact of teacher congeniality and friendliness and a thorough understanding of the subject matter that is to be covered, a charming personality, excellent communication abilities, and a sense of humor. (Later on in the

Guidebook this along with others will get much attention.)

- Morrison, N. (2014) publishes an article titled "Subject knowledge is the most important aspect of good teaching, according to experts," which contends and provides evidence that teachers' understanding of the subject is a significant factor in the learning of students. To read the article, type in your browser: "Morrison 2013 subject-knowledge.'

Lesson Design The Traditional Format

>> Ralph Tyler in 1949 authored an unassuming book titled Basic Principles of Instruction and Curriculum. It was well-received and was soon the standard design for the design of curriculum and lesson plans. Its main components included:

Objectives: What will the curriculum/lesson will allow students to accomplish.

- Organization: How the lesson or curriculum can be organized to maximize learning.

Learning Experiences: what the students will be taught to do so that they can achieve the stated goals.

- Verification of Effectiveness The processes (tests or demonstrations, etc.).) which demonstrate the effectiveness of the instruction efforts.

>> Madeline Hunter, in the 1970's and the 1980's, was able to surpass Tyler's method and became the leading authority on teaching organization and presentation. This is an 8 Step Lesson Design she advocated. It's still trendy.

1. Anticipatory Set: Teacher inspiringly introduces the subject, its purpose as well as its importance, along with the most significant elements.

2. Objectives: The teacher clearly explains what the students need expected to be able to do and why.

3. Input: The teacher takes the time to explain the material students need to learn , and then explains the students what they need to accomplish to achieve the goals.

4. Modelling. The teacher clearly demonstrates what the students should be doing.

5. Student Guided Training: They work with guidance from their teacher and observe.

6. Making sure students understand the material: The teacher is constantly circulating, observes and ensures that students comprehend the concepts they are learning.

7. Learning through Independent Practice: The students on their own take part in assignments and exercises to strengthen their learning.

8. The teacher concludes the lesson by addressing the lesson, asks students to ask

questions, gives feedback and tests or assesses the student's learning.

For more information about Hunter's suggestions, enter into your browser the phrase 'Hunter Leçon Plan.'

A Lesson Format that is More Recent called "Backward Design'

Grant Wiggins and Jay McTighe published a book in 2012 called Understanding by Design, in which they advocated for a brand new method of teaching and curriculum that is becoming more popular. Web Browser: Wiggins as well as McTighe 2012 . Understanding By Design.'

The method, often referred to as "backward design," asks teachers to first explain the students what, and on what basis student progress will be analyzed and analyzed. Students are then provided with instruction that assists them in achieving the desired outcomes.

This is similar to the use of the 'final exam to plan how to guide and assess students' learning, and then direct instruction to the test. Research suggests that the resulting learning is more complete and focused than is usually the norm.

The reverse design has an additional benefit it allows for 'formative assessment where teachers keep students informed of how they're progressing in meeting the goals they have set and not waiting until the end of the test to hear about the positive (or not-so-good) outcomes.

In the end, it is clear that when using the reverse design, you should carefully consider and communicate to students exactly what you would like students to understand, which is the things they'll need learn or perform on their the final test and the way they'll be instructed, assessed and assessed.

Effective Feedback, Rubrics and Feedback Instruction Enhancements

Enhancements, as it is referred to here, refers to factors that you can provide to enhance teaching and improve its effect. In this section, we will look at feedback and rubricsas two of the instructional enhancements highly suggested. Then, we'll bring attention to a range of other enhancements.

> Feedback. When teaching, feedback can be an extremely effective method of guidance that teachers use to keep their students in the right direction and to help them develop. This process includes specific responses by teachers to student's efforts including comments, examples or demonstrations to help students recognize, rectify their errors, and make advance.

In the past teachers would provide feedback after instruction was finished, usually by highlighting the mistakes made by students and providing suggestions on how to improve them (e.g., "You used the incorrect verb tense here. Use the subjunctive instead." or, "What do you think could be better done here? ?").

In the present, experts have found it is much more efficient for teachers to are able to identify whenever they can how students are performing wrong , and then aid them in making changes. This is known as feedback in formative or concept correction. It occurs when teachers are first able to spot mistakes made by students. It is thought to be extremely effective in helping students achieve quick, precise learning. Here are three tips on feedback you may want to keep in mind:

1. Effective feedback occurs if it is given within the immediate aftermath of an incident, rather than a few days or hours after.

2. Feedback is most effective when it concentrates on one thing at one time.

3. The process of feedback and guidance are significantly enhanced when utilized in conjunction with 'rubrics' which will be discussed in a moment.

In addition, feedback from teachers that is in the form of remarks like "great effort" or "improvement required" has been no more useful. Teachers are now advised to give whenever possible explicit evidence of the actions students have taken whether in a correct or incorrect manner and then encourage students to suggest improvements when they feel justified.

> Rubrics. Rubrics are visual guides that teachers give to aid students in finishing their assignments efficiently. It's been proven that rubrics, which accomplish what they say, are able to significantly enhance students' sense of purpose and performance:

1. Rubrics outline what students are to learn, do, and comprehend, which helps students to stay on the right track and reach their desired goals.

2. Rubrics allow students to assess their own progress towards attaining the goals they have set for themselves efficiently and effectively and, if necessary they reflect on how their efforts could be enhanced. To read more about the benefits and application of rubrics, enter into your browser the phrase 'rubrics for teaching.'

The Facet of 4 Jewels. Control of Subject Matter
Below are the four instructional "jewels that are related to curricula, subject matter and lessons

that will result in substantial improvement in the quality of learning.

Teacher displays strong understanding of the subject area

The teacher employs extremely effective instructional strategies

> The teacher emphasizes the "big big picture' during the start of each lesson

> Teacher provides rubrics and rubrics for direction and useful feedback.

The Previewing of 16 Ultra-Effective Aspects in Instruction

The present chapter concludes our preliminary discussion on the role of the Subject Matter and Curriculum Objectives, Subject Matter and other subjects in encouraging learning. To help you anticipate what's coming in this Guidebook, you should carefully review the below list of 16 super interventions in teaching. We've looked at some of them. These 16, which are presented without explanation, are self-explanatory.

- 4 highly effective Teachers Specific Characteristics

A Enticing Teacher

In-Depth Knowledge of Curriculum and Subject Matter

The ability to connect to and Motivate Students

Ability to communicate Very Well

\> 4 Great Methods for Teaching
Direct Instruction
Problem Solving
Class Discussion
• Reciprocal Teaching
\> 4 Effective Strategies of teaching
Piagetian Adjustments
Brain-Compatible Teaching
Conceptual Change Teaching

Backward Design Learning
\> 4 Superb Techniques of Teaching
Making Learning Expectations Clearly Detainable
Giving appropriate feedback at the appropriate time
Regular use of rubrics in Formative Evaluation and Instruction
- Regularly Involving Students in Concept Mapping
If you don't do more than use the previously mentioned 16 most effective elements of teaching, then you likely will be a great teacher. However, dear reader there's more to learn and more to be learned.
END OF FACET 2 INPUT - PLEASE PROCEED TO PRACTICUM 2

Practice 2 - Command of Curriculum, Subjects and lessons

Warm-up Quiz

Choose the suitable option to complete each question. ('Correct answer' is not given. Discussion with other learners is it is possible.)

1. A Facet of Teaching just completed appears to pay the least focus to the following: the following:) superior teachers as well as the curriculum,) curriculum (c) instruction, and d) attitude of students

2. Teachers who are exceptional possess high levels of A) personal sensitiveness to the needs of their students, (b) admiration from a mutual source as well as the c) understanding of the subject matter and the d) intelligence

3. A leading authority in the field of curriculum development:) B. F. Skinner B. F. Skinner, B. F. Skinner,) Harry Wong, c) Marvin Marshall, d) Ralph Tyler

4. A teacher issue that is not covered in the Facet 1.) instruction or instruction, the second) cooperation between parents and teachers (c) bigger image and the d) the subject matter component

5. From the list below, they are generally the most unreliable in the teaching process of the following: A) facts or data, theorists,) theories

and theories, theory,) principles and the d) assumptions

6. Skills for manipulating and understanding subjects are: a) inherent abilities and as well as) learned abilities that are the latter being) ineffective for teachers and students, (d) exactly the same thing as motivation

7. The content of the current school curricula are likely to be heavily determined by:) Teachers as well as the curriculum,) textbooks and c) parents, and d) test of achievement

8. It is not essential for a great teacher The most important thing is: It is not essential to a) using the night oil and the burning of midnight oil,) the subject matter of knowledge and C) good communication and D) engaging with students

9. The 1980s are the decade with the most influential authority in the organization of lessons It was: the following:) Madeline Hunter, b) John Dewey, c) Jean Piaget, d) J. J. Rousseau

10. The "backward design" involves mainly the following: the following:) traditional curriculum and (b) lesson planning and (c) notes of the learning the steps that are the d) communication between parents

Your personal 7-point summary of Facet 2

Determine what you consider to be the seven most significant concepts or ideas that are presented on this Facet. Based upon your perceptions, perform these three actions:

1. Sort your choices by the effect you think they will impact learning
2. Make sure you can define each of them in your own terms
3. Discuss and compare your findings with your fellow learners

Knowledge of Subject Matter Vocabulary, Goals and Concepts

In relation to Subject Matter generally make sure that you are aware of these words:

Big picture: facts theories, concepts and hypotheses.

~ Procedures: categorizing, recognizing, interpreting, organizing

~ Value: appreciation, enjoyment, satisfaction

Then, for the subject you are teaching or expecting to teach:

In two paragraphs define the nature of the subject and value

Identify three key concepts or themes that are that are suggested in this Facet

Identify and describe the particular aspects highlighted in this Facet that you will likely to use

Three of them which are your personal most cherished

Concerning the Curriculum

In the case of a subject that you teach or are planning to teach, you should discuss with your fellow students the following aspects: its nature, purpose and essential characteristics, how it can benefit both teachers and students and how students can be taught it.

Concerning Subject Matter, Curriculum Element, and Relationships

Concept Map One-Page A single sheet of paper, create an idea map of the key components within this Facet. Draw connections between the elements. Create a presentation that is appealing memorable, memorable, and simple to follow. (For many different kinds of graphic mapping styles use the search term 'concept mapping' to the search bar of your Internet web browser.)

• Practice using Your Concept Map Utilize your concept map to describe using your own language, the meaning and significance of the data you've included. Try to be clear and maintain a logical flow. Learn with other learners and save your idea diagram for future use and to review.

> Useful Application: Begin to create practical plans for the inclusion in your teaching style the principles you like or methods of instruction described on this Facet. Join your peers to exchange valuable thoughts and observations.

Learn to master the subject matter you are studying

For a topic or subject area that you teach or anticipate or plan to teach, consider these questions to improve your understanding, and ultimately students' comprehension of what you'll be teaching and what your students will be able to be learning. If you can, do these activities with other learners:

Cognitive components The cognitive components: look over the overall picture, its significance and the four main concepts to be understood.

> Skills components: delineate and describe the steps you'd like to instruct your students in order to assist them in learning the new concepts.

• Affective component: state what you'd do to help students comprehend the importance of what they're learning and how they can appreciate the value of what they are learning.

Expand vocabulary: Identify five terms that you like students to know and then explain how you can assist them in learning these terms.

Off the cuff: Ensure that you are able to anytime, discuss the following about the subject(s) you are teaching in general terms: the nature of the subject and its overall importance and value; five major themes that are relevant to the subject(s) as well as five key applications and ten of the most crucial facts, ideas or practices.

Useful for Purpose

Start preparing workable plans to include in your teaching style at minimum seven of the suggestions for instruction included on this Facet. Join with learners to exchange observations and ideas.

Exercise in the area of Expansion

For a week, dedicate 2 hours per day studying as much as in a way that is compatible with the subject and the skills you will be teaching. Note your learning efforts and then share your findings with your teaching partners. Do not forget about this exercise!

END OF FACET 2 - PLEASE PROCEED TO FACET 3

Facet 3: You align instruction with your Brains of Your Students

Your objective is to learn how brains of children develop and function in different levels of development, and secondly, how their brains learn the best, and how to most effectively teach them.

Why this topic is crucial

Human learning in all its forms is dependent on the brain and its functions. In order to be able to teach the most effective way it is essential to understand the way that students' brains work at different phases of growth, what brains can and can't accomplish, what they require and want as well as what triggers them most effectively, what they try to avoid, the different emotions they feel and, most importantly, the way they learn and recall. When you understand these aspects and understandings, you can ensure that all the information you impart is presented in a way that increases the ability of students to process, store as well as enjoy and utilize information.

Brain Development in Students of Capabilities, Preferences and Preferences

The primary goal for the Guidebook is to guide you to become an extremely efficient teacher. In order to achieve that it is vital to know the way that students' brains work as well as what they're capable of and not able to do as well as how they can best learn, comprehend and retain. Be aware that teachers actually teach the brains of our students. The more we know about the way that brains function to function, the more we can assist them in their learning.

In the past we were able to learn a lot about the brain's process of learning and memory. With the constant developments in brain research, we know these things better and we can effectively teach. To help you gain and utilize that knowledge we'll now look at an overview of how students' brains are incredibly developed perform, study, recall to create, solve issues and interact with fellow learners efficiently and happily.

What are the Basics of Human Brain Development

Cerebral neuron (microscopic neurons in the brain) begin to form soon in human embryos. Within four to five weeks of conception, they're dividing extremely quickly and by birth, they will be at most 100 billion. This is about 14 times the amount of human beings living on Earth. Before birth, the majority of these neurons will have developed some or all synapses (connection to other neurons) which allow the exchange of information. Synapses are formed rapidly and frequently, and are strengthened by experience and reflection.

The early years of childhood are a fascinating time in the development of the brain However, for our purposes here , we'll skip to the school years of early childhood. In this time our brains have made enormous leaps in the development of language and human capabilities that is far superior to the capabilities of communication in every other animal species. But, however precocious the brain is however, it is unable to think rationally until about seven. At that point, it begins to recognize causes-effect relationships and the relationship between means and ends however, only when thinking is based on 'mental images' of objects and actions. Abstract reasoning does not develop until a few years later from the time you reach 11 years old, the age when students begin to think and reason more clearly.

As the brain develops, subtle changes continue to occur within the brain until it becomes fully developed, which is usually around the 20s to early to mid 20s. But even after that the brain continues to be influenced by a variety of experiences, by storing information through interaction with other individuals as well as engaging in productive and reflective thinking.

A Brain's Complements: What they Like and How They Work

In this case, please make use of the Internet browser to visit the "thinking brain tour for business or another similar website which provides a comprehensive visually-oriented tour through the human brain including descriptions of the places and functions of the major components. The URL is: http://www.thethinkingbusiness.com/brainzone/brain-tour. Look at the following three regions that comprise the brain

> Brain stem, also known as the 'reptilian brain,' that is the center of awareness, alertness, and awareness. It regulates blood pressure and breathing. It also handles issues of self-defense, survival and signals of possible danger (responses commonly are referred to as freeze or fight).

> Limbic System or 'mid-brain it is the home of pleasure, emotions and pleasure, as well as some memory for the long term, biorhythms and social bonds. It also regulates motivation, memory for long-term, and certain kinds of behaviour.

> Cerebral cortex or the 'upper brain', which is the brain's primary location for cognitive processes like logic, language creative thinking, decision-making as well as information processing. It is often referred to as 'the brain that thinks.'

The left part in the brain (sometimes called the logical mind) is primarily responsible for part of our body's right. It concentrates on languages, lists, numbers analysis, logic, and other analyses.

The left part of our brain (sometimes called the creative brain) is more likely to control that left-hand side. It is primarily concerned with rhythm color, spatial awareness, imagination and creativity, dimensions and the whole-body awareness.

Take note of the amygdala, which is an area of tissue inside the temporal region right in front of the eye. It is believed that it senses the dangers, manage emotions, trigger the survival instincts and control memory, though the mechanism behind these actions isn't yet understood.

In the ago, much was made about the main roles of the right and left brain hemispheres incorrectly implying that both hemispheres function somewhat independently. Although each exerts different influences, both hemispheres are constantly sharing information and function together. The old practice of instructing one hemisphere in contrast to the other is now to be valid.

The Brain's Amazing capabilities

The neocortex in the brain is the place where you can find higher cognitive functions like thought language, learning, and language. The brain is made up of about 20 billion brain cells (Brain Statistics and Facts 2014) It is the area of the brain that worries the most with learning, but other areas are also involved.

To help you see dendrites, cerebral neurons, synapses, and axons input into your browser the words "neuron images. This will bring pictures of neuronal cells nuclei, dendrites and Axons, and the axon's endpoints.

Enter'synapse images then you'll be able to see images of the places in which information travels between neurons. Every single brain's neuron can connect to other neurons through structures known as "synapses. The theory is that every neuron could theoretically create as many as 10,000 synapses. This could provide us trillions of synapses in the brain. We can't imagine a figure as large, however, we are aware that it's a staggering amount and gives a sense of the real and possible capabilities of the brain.

It's fascinating that when we turn three, we are blessed with a hundred trillion synapses in our brains however by the time we reach adolescence around half of them are eliminated, for reasons that aren't yet fully understood. Another fascinating discovery concerns the length of all brain's blood vessels, which feed the brain's vast amount of cells. Estimates of the length of these vessels vary between 100,000 and 172,000 km in one brain. Most of these vessels are tiny. For more details on the brain, read the CEU Group's Facts About the Human Brain (2016). The information it provides is truly incredible.

The development of synapses within every brain area is heavily influenced by our daily experiences. It begins in the very beginning by interactions with other people and playtime, as well as verbal interactions and rhymes, rhythms and physical activities that we engage in actively.

In our beginning years, there is a start within the brain an process known as myelination. Myelin is a white fatty tissue that is deposited in the axons as it wraps around them. Its function isn't yet understood, but some theories suggest that it assists in transmitting signals more quickly. Myelination starts in the sensory and motor regions within the brain (the brain cortex and the stem) and then gradually moves forward into the areas that regulate memory, thought and emotions.

In the adolescent years the brain undergoes further restructuring, but this will not be completed until early to mid-20s, by when the brain is capable of thinking in a way that is adult-like (Your Teenager's Developing Brain 2014).

As it is undergoing this change, the brain eliminates a number of synapses that are not being utilized, while enhancing the ones that are currently being utilized and adding more as required. The process starts in the rear of the brain and gradually moves towards the prefrontal cortex, which is the part of the brain that is responsible for making decisions. While the prefrontal cortex still developing in teens cerebral cortexes, amygdala has an important role in making decisions and solving issues. The amygdala also regulates emotions and impulses. These could explain teenagers their tendency to act impulsively and not think rationally.

To gain a better understanding of the brain of an adolescent and its influence on behavior and thinking Take a moment to read the fantastic 2009 Internet article written by Linda Chamberlain entitled "The Amazing Adolescent Brain: What Every Teacher and Youth Service Professional and Healthcare Provider Should know." (Type into the browser : Chamberlain's what every educator must be aware of.') This information is mostly about the brains of teenagers can be particularly useful for teachers working with teens. Based on this article and others of the same kind it is possible to draw the following conclusions regarding adolescent thinking:

1. Teenagers think about information differently as adults do, especially in the way they organize and prioritize information.

2. There are some functional differences between male and female brains. Female brains, which have greater gray matter are typically better at verbal abilities as well as information processing. Brains of males, which have greater white matter are better in problem-solving and spatial awareness. The hippocampus also is more prominent in females in their early years which could explain more social skills. However, in males , the amygdala as well as hypothalamus grow larger, possibly contributing to a greater desire for sexual pleasure as well as assertiveness, an interest in contact sports and the inability to remain still for long periods of time. In general, the female brain develops more quickly than that of males.

3. Teenagers haven't yet completed the process of developing an ability to judge or have the ability to control their impulses. They see danger differently as adults do and are more susceptible to take risks, especially with other teenagers.

4. The teenagers to surround themselves with loving, caring adults who are aware of anxiety, risk-taking and rule-bending, and who provide a thoughtful and caring direction that eases stress and allows students to make better choices.

The way the brain learns

Now let's review the way that the brain learns, and some of the important educational factors involved in the learning process:

> It takes to organize and take in information. The brain is selectively attuned to the information it receives via its senses and manipulates it by varying ways, including:

It stores information. It Stores Information. Brains store (remembers) huge quantities of information in various forms like visual impressions and vocal sounds, melodies emotional expressions, language connections, odors, flavors routines, habits and other procedures.

It creates meaning and gains Understanding. The brain is always trying to understand and increase meaning, which means that it seeks to find the meaning of the world, and in doing so , we are able to look over who, what and when, as well as to what, how and the result (the domain of thinking).

> It is able to apply and generate Information. The brain is prone to apply (to utilize the information it holds) and organize information to ensure greater accessibility and efficiency and change information to create patterns that are new, concepts use, explanations, and solutions.

It is a process that changes as you get older. The brain's abilities aren't forever fixed. They evolve throughout life through the growth of new synapses as well as the strengthening of neural pathways by maturation, learning, sensory stimulation, behaviour and language as well as emotions. The brain's capacity for growing its capabilities to learn over long time periods is known as neuroplasticity.'

Teaching in a "Brain-Compatible" Manner

Numerous authorities have investigated ways of providing instructions that enhances the brain's abilities to retain, learn and utilize information.

Renate Caine as well as Geoffrey Caine (1997) were the first this by using a formalized process they first called 'Brain-based learning which is now referred to as Natural Learning. For a look at the implications of their work, read Caine and the Caine's 12-point Brain/Mind Natural Learning Principles, that have attracted worldwide attention and are included in the curriculum of many schools.

These 12 principles are loaded with practical implications for teaching. Enter in your search engine "Caine and caine's twelve Brain/Mind natural learning principles.'

A Short Aside on what we know about the exact factors that triggers the brain during learning.

Neuroscientists have developed procedures for monitoring electrical and metabolic activity in the brain, using electroencephalography (EEG) to observe electrical activity, and brain scans to observe blood flow and metabolism of glucose and oxygen. When one observes EEG as well as blood flow at the same time one can observe that new information flows rapidly across the cortex's input regions into the activation of the reticular system which regulates consciousness and the ability to concentrate attention. It also connects to the limbic system that regulates emotions and memory.

Strangely enough, the amygdala sometimes blocks this process. It reacts to anxiety and anxiety by blocking the flow of information, making it more difficult for brains to store the information and make it easier to process. It also reduces the degree that emotions influence learning. It helps us realize that students do not learn as efficiently through coercion, and more effectively when they are in a state of trust, confidence, and positive emotions.

Aiding students' Brains Store and Retrieve Memories

Intellectual development is facilitated by the generation of memories that are stored over time. If a particular experience is enough to establish an neuronal pathway that involves at least two neurons, the neurons can exchange information and link up to other neurons. When these pathways grow in their capacity to store information that is new or improve its accuracy the person is said to have learned new processes and information.

If the learning is able to be later recalled whenever needed, it's believed to have entered the long-term memory which is where it's usually accessible throughout the course of. However, if the neural pathway fails to reach an appropriate level of development or isn't activated frequently, we often do not have the capacity to recall the information into the consciousness level however certain triggers can cause it to return. If the memory is associated with extremely strong emotions, like fear or excitement, the neuronal pathway could be permanently locked to the memory for the duration of this one event alone.

The Adolescent Brain

Principal of the middle school Peter Lorain (see his 2013 Internet article titled 'Development of young adolescents: Good News for Middle School Teachers') draws attention to the growing growth of the brains of adolescents previously believed to reach peak performance around 15, but which is now understood to continue developing until the 20s and beyond. Find out what Lorain states about adolescents in relation to:

> Continuous development. The ability to develop their abilities to apply critical thinking, problem-solving, organizing, and controlling impulses

• Intense Interests. Their preference is for activities that involve other peers

Attention Limitation. The inability to focus on more than a handful of information that are new at any moment

> Variety. They prefer different lessons that include many hands-on and interactive activities

> Stimulation. The intense, positive emotions they experience with extremely stimulating experiences

Concept Connections. Students need help in connecting information they learn with their previous experiences

> Discussions. The importance in students' interaction with peers in the process of acquiring and making use of information that is new

> Effective Routines. The ability to be more effective in the context of routines and expectations that are consistent.

Aiding the brain to maximize learning

These are some instructional strategies you can employ to boost the longevity and quality of learning for students.

> Increase Involvement in Sensory. Create learning experiences that continually require multiple sensory inputs and not just those of hearing, sight as well as smell and taste and touch, but also the senses of body posture and motion.

> Novelty and intrigue in Feature. Combine intrigue, novelty and surprise emotions, and even difficulties into learning activities. These elements stimulate attention, stimulating the brain and aid in the formation of neural patterns of greater complexity.

> Involve Physical Activity. Include physical activity in your teaching activities. The brain appears to be particularly sensitive and capable of storing and recall information with physical activity. active in rhythms, melodies and interactive games such as acting, singing as well as role-playing and the similar.

• Facilitate Cooperative Learning. Brains seem to be eager to connect with one another and appear to be more effective in learning when they do it. Teaching can maximize learning by offering co-operative activities in small groups, during where students exchange ideas as well as organize and express their opinions as well as provide feedback and work together on projects.

> Teach Metacognitive and Cognitive Strategies. Cognitive strategies for learning involve keeping track of the main elements, summarizing reasoning, describing the information in one's own words making conclusions, and re-reading. Metacognitive strategies involve planning a plan for learning, identifying the skills needed and strategies, and preparing to assess one's understanding of texts, planning for self-assessment, self-correction and self-assess and deciding on how to assess the progress towards completing the task.

• Use Rubrics to Aid in Learning. Rubrics, as mentioned earlier are concise visual representations of the things students should be able to know, including effective methods and standards of quality and benchmarks to indicate the progress made. They are particularly useful when students work in small groups and in groups of smaller size and also when they are monitoring and evaluating their own progress.

• Provide helpful feedback. Like we mentioned earlier feedback in learning and teaching is the process of giving feedback to students on the actions they take in order to learn. It's a great strategy to boost performance, and it is more effective when it is exchanged between the students and teachers (two-way feedback). Effective feedback is both educational and positive and includes indications of the actions that one is doing, and it could or could not be optimal or accurate.

After getting feedback from the brain, it evaluates the information it receives according to its levels of interest, accuracy and the potential worth. If the feedback is judged to be insignificant or not worth the effort then it is generally ignored. If it is considered important, beneficial or fun the feedback is likely to be absorbed into your long-term memory. The brain will then automatically link this new information with the existing knowledge.

Teachers can improve the efficacy and effectiveness of their feedback by asking the students "What is your knowledge of this subject?" Or, "What can be I able to do in my efforts to assist you to to understand this subject more clearly?"

• Allow for periods of Reflection. Help students consider the information they're learning and allow them the time to reflect on their learning. This provides their brains with the chance to reflect and evaluate gaps, fill in the gaps and ask questions, organize information, and contemplate the what next steps to take. The philosopher John Dewey, an early advocate of the concept of activity-based learning claimed that we don't gain as much knowledge from participating in an activity, as we do by later looking back on the event.

Learning to align with the brain's preferences

You've seen how the brain naturally equipped and inclined to be able to comprehend and remember, to make sense of things, resolve issues, and even create. It develops by engaging in different activities, and then looking back on the experiences. It is possible to improve your teaching by taking these factors into consideration when working with students:

• Developmental Stages. Instructing should be compatible with the students' capacities at various levels of development.

The Brain's Preferences. Help the brain do what it is able to do best. In normal situations it is engaged in a heightened way with what it considers to be fascinating, personal important, personal or a part of physical or emotional experiences. It is inclined to ignore non-personal information.

> Feeling of Safety. In the school environment brains function at their optimally when students feel secure and protected in a symbiosis of calm, enjoyment and optimism, a determination and good humor.

Sensory Involvement. The brain craves stimulation that stimulates its own natural processes of learning.

> Acceptance and Association. The brain appears to gain from close relationships with other brains in situations where personal danger is not too high. Therefore, when you can create a group environment, you can encourage group work as well as cooperation and teacher-student interaction. Inspire students to view each other as socially equal which is evident in friendships, friendships and personal respect, as well as the how they treat each other and in inclusive group activities. Instruct students that each member of the class is changing and learning, and can be supported to advance to the extent they are able, and that co-operation and consideration towards one another is beneficial to all.

> Best Learning Environments. The brain is most effective in environments of optimism or pleasure as well as moderate difficulty. It appears to gain the most from instruction delivered in brief periods of stimulating input and activities that are which are followed by a couple of minutes contemplation and reflection where students consider the implications, meanings and possible uses of the learning they have learned.

> Undesirable Learning Conditions. The brain doesn't learn in times of emotional or physical anxiety, boredom, stress or overload, negative thinking, or pessimism.

> > The Big Picture. As we've mentioned before it is believed that the brain is more adept at absorbing the information faster when pupils are presented with the larger picture of what they have to be learning about, its purpose as well as the reasons for its importance and how it is structured and what it allows one to accomplish. Big picture introductions are able to are more effective and lasting results when they are they are accompanied by diagrammatic presentations as well as examples of work performed by students in other classes and anticipations of upcoming classes.

> Follow The Big Picture. After explaining the big picture, proceed to other details or activities that grab the brain's attention (e.g. fascinating facts, challenging problems or anecdotes, puzzles or fascinating questions). When you're done, let students participate in an activity that stimulates the brain, such as something sensory, auditory or kinesthetic or all of them.

> Remembering. Students are more likely to retain the information they are regularly

exposed to or they find particularly interesting, fun, or useful.

> Reassurance. It is important for students to know that you will continue to engage them in activities that are enjoyable and enhance their sense of wellbeing, enhance their knowledge, expand new avenues of thinking and increase their capacity to tackle new challenges and deal with issues. Stress your students that the brains of their children are constantly evolving, learning and getting better with each new thing they are taught.

In the End: A Brief Summary of how to teach students' brains

The brain develops in phases, each of which it displays certain abilities and preferences. However the brain is trying to stay clear of anything that it finds boring, dangerous or uncomfortable, however, it is constantly seeking and definitely enjoys stimulation from sensory stimuli curiosity, novelty, as well as positive relationships with other people (verbal as well as intellectual and social). For the best teaching experience ensure that you know the stages of development in the brain as well as what students are able to do and not do at each stage process, and the ways in the brain processes information and organizes it, recalls it solving problems, and creates an environment, and more importantly, how it is most effectively taught.

Four Jewels of Facet 3, Alignment to the Brain

> Be sure to align teaching with the brain's preferences of students and their abilities

> Create learning environments that students will enjoy

Utilize activities to aid the brain in learning how to store and recall information.

• Provide practice for learning, problem solving, and reasoning

END OF FACET 3 INPUT - PLEASE PROCEED TO PRACTICUM 3

Practicum 3. Modifying Instruction to Students"Brains

Do your best to find an aspiring teacher to join you in exchanging and interpreting ideas about teaching the brain.

Warm-up Quiz

Choose the most suitable option to complete each of the statements.

1. Neuroplasticity in the brain refers to the following: an) the atomic structure, b) molecular nature,) inflexibility and the) the capacity in learning over time.

2. The brain region called'reptilian"is t:) the brain stem the brain stem,) amygdala,) central cortex and the d) the occipital region

3. The time at when the brain is at its most attuned to learning to speak The brain is most in tune with language learning) early 20s and then) mid-teens (c) 2-7 years old, (d) pre-birth

4. Memories are kept in brain in the form of the following: the following:) verbalizations) images or images, (c) movement kinetics and D) senses

5. In the majority of people the dominant hemisphere the brain is a) left and right) right and C) central and dorsal,) dorsal

6. Children begin to think abstractly by the age of A) seven, and b) eleven, c) fourteen. d) nineteen.

7. The amount of neurons in the brain of a baby relative to the adult's brain, is the following: the number of neurons is:) roughly the identical number, the difference is b) smaller,) higher d) not confirmed

8. The area of the brain where teaching is frequently directed is: A) brain stem and B) corpus collosum the c) the occipital lobe, and d) prefrontal cortex

9. The primary goal of formal education is to be able to) retain information and the b) comprehend information and to) take pleasure in or use information, and d) describe the meaning of information

10. Teenage brains are different from adult brains in the following areas: a) neuroplasticity

and the b) prefrontal development and the) number of neurons d) the length of blood vessels

Terminology Review

Review and increase your knowledge of the following brain-related subjects and the impact on your teaching the prefrontal cortex; the stages of development in the brain; strength and weaknesses at different levels; short-term memory; long-term memory; effects of emotions on learning activities; brain-friendly environments as well as learning, understanding recalling and applying, creating and neuroplasticity.

7-Point Summary

Write on a single page what you think to be the seven most important concepts or insights that you came across during this Facet. Discuss and exchange ideas with other students.

Understanding the Implications for Teaching

Be sure to present to your complete satisfaction these concepts as well as the implications for teaching

> Disposition to Learn. Your brain naturally inclined to learn. This it learns through experience and reflection. Are there implications for teaching?

> Interaction with Others. The brain seems to delight and gain from interaction with other

brains. This has led experts to describe the brain as'social and social in the natural world. Are there implications for teaching?

• Stages of development. The brain develops in distinct stages until it is fully adult functioning around the 20s to early 20s (previously thought to be at around 15 years old). Each stage is defined by certain limitations and abilities. The implications for teaching, specifically at the level you would like to teach at?

• The learning Process. The brain learns by recognizing events and, when it is it is possible, linking them to memories already stored within the brain. Also, it learns through introspection contemplation, reflection, and imaginative thinking. These processes help build concepts thoughts, memories, and abilities that are controlled by the brain's "executive functions', such as noting and recognizing, sorting, connecting and implementing. Are there implications for teaching?

Conditions that enhance learning. Learning happens best in educational conditions that are stimulating, enjoyable curiosity, excitement, creativity, and problem-solving. It is able to be boosted by physical exercise or multi-sensory input. certain music, rhythms as well as graphic arts. However learning can be hindered by the negative atmosphere and stress, as well as rejection and boredom. What are the implications for teaching?

> The Brain's Ability to Understand. As the brain absorbs more information, it tries to comprehend (grasp the meaning and information of) the information it has absorbed however, it might require help in doing this. Implications?

> Short-Term Memory. Normally, the short-term memory of the brain can store at any time 3 or 4 bits of information, which is about half of what we used to think. Additionally, the majority of the information that is stored will be gone in thirty seconds, or even less, if the brain is not experiencing emotions or perform activities that transform the information into long-term memory. The implications for teaching?

> Long-Term Memory. The information stored in long-term memory can be accessed in conjunction with mental images emotional, melodies smells, procedural patterns, lists, as well as fragments of language, such as rhymes and games on words. What are the implications for teaching?

Nature and importance of Meaning. Meaning is defined as the importance of the comprehension of the connections between different concepts and experiences. It is demonstrated through the capacity to communicate or demonstrate the qualities, processes, implications and their uses. It is enriched or made more complicated by layering which is the addition of information to the patterns already stored in memory. Implications?

• Learning and Teaching. The brain is increasingly proficient in learning when it is constantly engaged with a focussed attention learning, processing, practice memory, problem solving and reminiscing. Implications?

• Reliability and reliability of Memory. Memory isn't as reliable as previously believed. It's a flexible thing and is easily changed due to new experience. To ensure that we remember the information accurately it is important to regularly reflect on the lessons we have learned. Implications?

The Brain is unique. While all brains develop and function the same way, .o two brains are the same. This is a strong indication that no two students can learn or process information in precisely the same way. This Guidebook we will look at the aspects that apply to learners and teachers generally. There are always exceptions and many of them. Implications?

personal relevance and learning. Judy Willis (2014b), an expert on teaching to the brain, says that learning can be improved when learning experiences in the classroom are pertinent to students' interests, lives and interests. Relevance makes lessons more engaging and challenging without being overwhelming, thus lessening boredom and anxiety. Implications?

Special Techniques. Activities that are often beneficial in the process of learning include story telling, role-playing as well as art, music and poetry. Implications?

> Aligning Teaching and brain functions. Students are more successful when teachers are able to align their teaching with brain abilities. Implication?

> The mastery of goals and objectives. In order to improve the learning process, instructors are encouraged to help students regularly practice previously learned skills, content and concepts to ensure that the information is absorbed and is retained in their long-term memory systems. To prevent boredom, mix up the tasks and, if appropriate, add graphic design, music poetry, drama as well as role-playing and creative writing.

> Evaluation and Feedback and Evaluation. Students do better when they get - while working on a specific task - constructive feedback from their teachers or teacher-

prepared rubrics which specify the tasks students must complete. Implications?

• Application of Learning. Teaching is successful in the way that it improves retention over time and allows students to apply or apply what they've learned. Implications?

One-Page Concept Map

Create a concept map of one page of the information contained on Facet 3. Indicate the content and connections. Create a memorable presentation. (For help, type 'concept mapping' in your Internet browser.)

Practiceusing the Concept Map

Utilizing your concept map and your concept map, you can explain, first before you to yourself and later to others, your most favorite ideas in the Facet as well as how they can contribute to efficient teaching.

Useful for Purpose

As we have said, the information offered within this Facet is only of worth unless you are able to use it effectively in classroom situations. So, try to develop a plan that is feasible to implement at least seven of the concepts or strategies discussed through this Facet. Connect with at least one of your fellow students to exchange valuable information and observations. of ideas.

Chapter 6: Offer An Excellent Learning

Environment

YOUR GOAL: To organize and manage your space for learning in a way that will help students excel at the classroom.

Learning Locations

We've mentioned the fact that learning venues are physical surroundings in which learning and teaching take place, including gyms, classrooms, shops, and so on. When they're at their best these venues contribute significantly to high-quality teaching and enjoyable learning.

In the coming weeks, we'll look at the essential elements of venues, how they can do and how they can be most efficiently managed, created and maintained. Although there is a bit of research about venues, the best guidance comes from experienced teachers and reputable experts in the field of education and learning.

The nature of Superior Venues

One of your primary teaching responsibilities is to make sure that the learning spaces that you create contribute to the process of learning. You can accomplish this by organizing your classrooms, optimizing them, and managing your spaces to meet your the needs of students as well as your own needs. As a result, you'll be asked to do what is necessary to ensure your students are exposed to the following characteristics of top learning environments:

• Safety Comfort as well as Stimulation. These characteristics help to make learning more enjoyable as they make students more comfortable and encourage interaction between the class members.

> Feeling of acceptance and belonging. This helps students feel accepted, valued and valued.

> All-Over Ambience of Positivity. The best places are filled with a sense of optimism positive, excitement, optimism positive energy, support and achievement. You need to develop and keep these traits as well as at the at the same time, minimize, or even remove from your classes any negative tinges or pessimism. Also, you must avoid inconsiderate behaviour.

• Abundant Sensory Input. Superior facilities offer high-quality auditory and visual conditions and activities that help students develop their sensations of touch and movement that in turn dramatically enhance retention and promote learning.

> Enjoyable Instruction. This is a quality that increases when you bring fun to the teaching process by engaging your students physically

physically, and mentally in engaging discussions, interactions and important instructional activities.

Physical Aspects of Quality-Learning Facilities

> Gail Senter (2012), teacher educator and author, provides these tips for creating quality learning spaces:

• For Ambience. Think about providing supporting colors, graphic or art display, special lighting and background music on occasion and other extras that students appreciate.

• for Work Space. Organise efficient seating areas, media spaces, work areas and teacher stations traffic patterns, and accommodating for students who have disabilities.

For Seating Arrangements. Give flexibility to students that allow them to work in groups , and allow you to move around quickly. For ideas on seats, just type "optimal seating for classrooms in your browser. To view the latest developments in furniture for classrooms enter into your browser "classroom furniture' and you'll discover a wide range of products that are distinct from the typical rows of desks for students.

• for Wall Space. You might want to consider the use of white boards, bulletin boards chart areas, display areas or maps (if utilized) and area for visual projection, as well,, if needed spaces for displays of the work of students.

To use as Countertop Space. If you have the space, think about displaying the equipment that is special, such as globes, models, kits and special purpose tools and even aquaria or terraria.

• Mark Phillips (2014), journalist and teacher, offers an entirely different list of ideas for maximising the potential of your spaces. Check out his brief but powerful Internet article, 'A Place for Learning: The Physical environment of Classrooms. If you type into your browser 'Phillips's Physical Classroom Management', you will be presented with a variety of suggestions on satisfaction, morale, as well as high-quality interactions. Phillips suggests that whenever you can, involve students in creating and maintaining a high-quality classroom, which will give them a sense participation and makes them imagine the class as a group of learners. Phillips's comments on tables, desks and their placement will give you an idea to consider, and you'll appreciate the advice he gives about creating a pleasant environment to the instructor.

Researchers Peter Barrett, Yufan Zhang, Joanne Moffat, and Khairi Kobbacy (2013) performed extensive studies of learning environments in an attempt to identify what elements of physical environments are most effective in facilitating learning for students. They found that interior lighting to be particularly important as they found that students exposed to natural, broad spectrum lighting are able to learn more effectively than those who study who are in areas lit by cool-white fluorescent light.

Some experts suggest that soft colors in the interior have an impact on learning. This is also true for background music in certain situations (although the quieter settings are ideal for tasks that require a lot of concentration). Aromas can also enhance learning and boost memory (olfactory input goes directly into the brain's limbic system and aids in establishing vivid memories). Physical movement, when used in the right way is also a great way to improve memory and learning. This is, for example, when students perform the procedures they're learning.

Superior Venues Adapt to the Students' Needs and traits

>> Jean Piaget (1951), A Swiss development psychologist, who was previously cited in the past, offered valuable details on how students grow in their intellectual development and what they look in emotional and behavioral

terms throughout their developmental phases. Here's a short outline of his findings, which are highly respected to this day:

Primary Grades (Ages 5-8). Children are extremely active and require to move around a quantity. They do not differentiate between play and work and need to rest frequently. They are particularly interested as well as learning about art, music rhythms, stories, and other activities that involve movements.

Intermediate Grades (Ages 9-11). Students at this stage are becoming more capable of working independently and work in groups and appreciate each other's company. They are particularly drawn to learning that requires interaction and movement.

middle school grades (Ages 12-14). At this stage students can independently and as a group with their peers with no constant supervision from teachers. Teachers are able to interact with students in a mature way, and quickly establish cooperative relations with students. Students display respect and appreciation for teachers with the most advanced knowledge, understanding and courtesy.

Primary School Grades (Ages 15-18). In the majority of cases teachers engage with students as adults. Students view teachers as role models and mentors and are generally happy to see teachers treat them as peers.

Superior venues are not able to compete with their effective emotional tone

Tone is the atmosphere of emotionality that is present within the class. It can have a profound impact on the student's behavior and their learning. Many experts have provided valuable advice for improving the atmosphere in the classroom. Take a look at the following suggestions:

\>\> Terry L. Shepherd (2013) states that students are attracted by and love working with teachers who show enthusiasm and optimism. It is highly recommended to check out his chapter 3 in pp. 25-35 in Lee Smith and Denise Skarbek's book Professional Teacher Dispositions: Additional Information on the Common Sense. This data, accessible via the Internet in 2019 is highly scholarly and instructive, and accessible. To access it, enter the following: https://books.google.com.au/books?isbn=1475 800541. The site lets you go through various Chapters within the book. Chapter 3 is highly recommended.

\>\> Marvin Marshall (2016), an expert on stress management, recommends that teachers establish high-quality classroom tone by incorporating choices, responsibility, positivity and optimism into every aspect of learning and teaching. Marshall has found these traits to be particularly effective in improving the morale of students and sustaining desirable behavior and encouraging the student's learning. To gain access to his wealth of ideas and suggestions visit MarvinMarshall.com which is the Internet portal for his significant contribution to civility and positivity in classrooms. Among these are some examples:

Regarding Choice. Marshall encourages teachers to let students to make good choices among the options they are offered, saying that students will always react more positively to options than to directives that are mandatory as well as the fact that students when given the opportunity to choose (from three or two acceptable alternatives) their tendency to see themselves as victims shifts to a feeling of confidence and self-confidence.

Concerning Responsibility. Marshall is also urging educators to "help students realize that they, as students, are responsible for their actions" and to assist them in "choosing positive paths to take". Marshall urges teachers to include students as collaborators in maintaining the classroom's quality and gives them an understanding of their role in their learning.

About Optimism, Positivity and Optimism. Marshall mentions the evidence for optimism's positive effects upon the heart, immune system and other body parts and functions. He argues that students' optimism and levels have been proven to be a predictor of academic achievement better than SAT scores. He believes that optimism and hope are able to be taught and learned and urges teachers to when they interact with their students, to ask "How do I respond to, respond to or express this positively?"

>> P. M. Forni (2006) on Civility and Considerate Conduct. Forni who was for many years Director for many years of The Civility Initiative at Johns Hopkins University has significantly aiding teachers to establish and maintain the atmosphere which promote civility and respect in the classrooms they teach. He defines civility as a blend of "courtesy and politeness kind, good manners, kindness fairness, decency and caring for the needs of others". The 25 rules of respectful conduct' will help you and your students well. The 'rules' are available via the Internet. Take a look. 3 of them:

Reward others in a positive manner

Be nice to everyone else.

Give and accept praise

Forni states that civility, respect, and politeness are the actions we can take to show respect for the needs of others as important as our own, a mindset which is a key factor in building positive relationships. He also says that presenting ourselves with respect aids teachers by allowing us to be more effective with colleagues and students. The more considerate and respectful we act according to him that the more likely we will be to build relationships that enhance your quality of life as well as the lives that of the students. Forni recommends that teachers talk about the issues with their students and to involve students in drafting the school's of conduct. of Civil Conduct, which may be as straightforward as this:

My goal is to always demonstrate respect for the other members of the Class by treating others respectfully and in a fair manner.

I will always try my best to be a better learner without affecting others in their efforts to learn. Then, Forni adds this advice to instructors: "Treat your students and communicate with them in the same way you would with your friends. We do not critique our peers and blame them or criticize them or them. Instead we listen, help and offer encouragement". For brief, captivating description of Forni's "Choosing Civility ideas, check out his Internet production, which is accessible through your web browser the following: Forni choosing civility pdf.

\>\> Michael Linsin (2013), on how to establish a high-quality class tone. Linsin is a well-known education writer, offers six suggestions you should do before meeting your students to establish a high-quality class tone. You can find his article by searching for 'Linsin's 6 Things You Need To Do on the First Day Of School' on your internet browser. This is a top piece of advice! Visit this site to see what he says about

~ Connections. Establishing personal connections from the moment both you and students set eyes.

~ Excellence. Instilling a culture of excellence through teaching students in detail how they can perform the tasks that are they are expected to do.

~ Fun. Explaining how you want to be a fun participant in the class and how the students can participate in a way that is appropriate.

~ Your Promise. A promise to your students that you will do everything you can to ensure that they get every chance to learn in school and be entertained while doing it.

~ Demonstrating. You must demonstrate how you'll keep your class free from interruptions that aren't warranted and other acts of disrespect.

~ Plunging In. Engaging in something that is educational on your first day in the class to demonstrate that you're dedicated to learning (making sure that the first class is extremely interesting and active).

> BrainyQuote is a website which provides a wide selection of inspiring quotes, many of which you may want to share with your students. To access them, simply type "BrainyQuote" into your browser. One of the most fascinating quotes for teachers is by Mahatma Gandhi. Gandhi states that the power you wield over students comes from two different sources: the first is the fear that students have of being punished. The second one is the love you have for your students, which, he states, is 1000 times more effective than punishment. This website can be highly recommended. Here are some additional quotes from other sources:

William James: "Pessimism leads to weakness, optimism brings power"

" Helen Keller: "Optimism is the belief that can lead to accomplishment. It is impossible to achieve anything without faith and hope."

• Zig Ziglar: "Positive thinking will allow you to do much better than the negative thought."

Superior venues emphasize civil, responsible behavior

>> P. M. Forni (2002 • 2006) In the previous article, P. M. Forni defines 'civility' to mean "showing respect for other people and their views". Forni believes that it is the hallmark of successful people and embodies the qualities of kindness, courtesy and good manners honesty, sincerity, and compassion. When we conduct ourselves with respect, Forni says, we enhance our lives as well as the lives of others more satisfying and enjoyable.

The advice of Forni will benefit yourself and students in a positive way. Try to promote the importance of civility in your classroom through discussions, examples, demonstrations and acknowledging others and listening, speaking with respect as well as expressing appreciation and acceptance and making a sincere apology. Forni (2002) provides many interesting quotes that praise qualities of good civility. Below are 3 quotes that you may want to have your students be discussing and thinking about:

"Rudeness is the weak's imitation of the strength of" Eric Hoffer

"We can choose what we do which means that we have the option to choose to be civil and gracious" -- Dwight Currie

- "Three aspects of human existence are essential First, you must be compassionate. The second is to be considerate and the third is to be kind" Henry James Henry James

> C.M. Charles (2012) in the field of Responsible Self-Conduct. Charles believes that self-control of students in a responsible manner opens the way for learning however, irresponsible behavior hinders not just one's own development as well as the learning of others, too. Charles says that self-conduct that is responsible means taking the actions that one believes to be appropriate and correct to the circumstances and people that are at hand. Unresponsible self-conduct means acting without considering the consequences they may impact the people at the time.

He lists a variety of student behavior that you may encounter while teaching. These are listed here in order of most frequent (and the least harmful) to the less frequent (but more dangerous in their impacts on learning and teaching). Additionally, he lists strategies that can be useful in changing students' self-defeating behaviours.

Inattention: Student is distracted and mind wandering. Teachers can be positive: they evaluates the the attractiveness of the topic as well as reassess their own instruction to ensure that the subject is compatible with the needs of the student; (for minor cases) teacher is with student at all times when a student is repeatedly infractions. teacher will ask the student in private whether there is any issue, and what the best way to address it.

Apathy - Student not taking part and not putting in the effort, and not caring. Positive Interventions: the teacher makes sure that the topic is relevant and relevant; makes sure it's aligned to the student's needs and interests as well as interacts with students. invites students to consider an appropriate behavior and then asks students to identify a particular problem and, if there is, how they can aid them.

Distracting talk that is not needed and disrupts instruction. Positive Interventions: Teacher reminds students of the code of civility asking the class what the reasons for excessive talking and, if the behavior is repeated, immediately remind students that their behavior is self-defeating. Follow with clarification of what is suitable (per Morrish, to be discussed in the future) Also, ask the student to think of an appropriate choice (per Marshall, to be discussed in the future).

• Moving around Student is seen rising and moving around in a manner that is not permitted. Positive Interventions: Ask whether you can assist and review the codes of conduct, review the procedures for the activity in question (per Wong & Wong, to be discussed later) and ask the students to indicate the severity of their conduct (per Marshall).

Angry at other students - Student causes trouble, teases, picks at and calls names. Positive Interventions: Review class code of civility; employ the direct method of corrective actions (per Morrish, to be discussed in the future) Have student determine their conduct (per Marshall, to be to be discussed).

Disrupting: Student shouts at others or uses profane language, and incites others. Positive Interventions: Review the code of conduct; ask person to state the severity of their conduct (per Marshall); provide an immediate instruction (per Morrish).

Lying - Student tells lies to gain personal benefits. Positive Interventions: Private conference with the student; student assisted in suggesting a better decision in the future; maintaining of a personal relationship between the teacher and the student.

• Stealing - Student steals items that belong to other people. Positive Interventions: private discussion with student; return the things taken; keeping of a positive relationship between teacher and the student.

Cheating - Student alters or falsifies work for personal gain. Positive Interventions: Private conference with student; a declaration to student what is to be expected in the future and maintaining contact with the student.

Sexual harassment: Improper gestures, innuendos or advances. Positive Interventions: stop the behavior right away to highlight that the behaviour is in violation of the rules of the class and norms of conduct As an option last resort, refer the your student to a school counselor.

Disobedience of authority Student argues with teacher, does not listen to teacher, becomes hostile. Positive Interventions: Have student take time out to think and sit down and talk to the student afterward to discuss possible options; work to build a stronger connection with the student.

A Activitiy that is malicious Student causes damage to the property of the school or other. Positive Interventions: calmly end the behaviour; request that the offending student fix the damage, as soon as possible; refer the student to the school counselor.

Agression - Student becomes aggressive, threatens, pushes or hits, and the bully. Positive Interventions: If the violence is not too serious and is not a major issue, you can direct correct (per Morrish) or ask the student to assess the level of behaviour (per Marshall); for repeated incidents or more serious situations you should refer the student to the school counselor.

\>\> Harry Wong and Rosemary Wong (2005) prefer to promote responsible behavior by educating students exactly what they need to conduct themselves during all classes. The Wongs are convinced that their efforts assist students to comply with their obligations and not clash with their teachers.

\>\> Ronald Morrish (2003) suggests an approach that is easy to follow to assist students in conducting their lives in a respectful manner. He suggests that students be involved in writing the three to four guidelines for respectable behavior during class. Students will then be taught to follow these rules until they learn to follow them without difficulty. If a student does break the rules, he or must do it again in a manner that is acceptable.

\>\> Marvin Marshall (2014) maintains that most students who are disruptive in the classroom are doing it knowingly and with a conscious intention, that is, they decide to behave the way they choose to behave. To assist students in making better choices regarding their behavior, Marshall teaches them four levels of classroom behavior which he refers to as the levels A, B C and D.

Niveau A (anarchy) is the most difficult, lowest level. This is the behavior that is disruptive and unruly including shouting and bullying or making snide comments about other people. Students are aware that such acts aren't acceptable.

Niveau B (bossiness) is the second lowest degree. It's behavior that's unconsiderate and disruptive, like speaking during study time and interrupting the teacher or classmates, and generally interrupting the learning of others in class. Students are aware that such actions aren't acceptable.

The level C (compliance) is considered to be acceptable, however just because the educator demands or requires the student to comply. Student behavior needs to be monitored continuously this can hinder learning and can be very stressful on teachers.

A level (doing what is right) is a vastly superior level. It is defined as the an attitude that students understand to be considerate and respectful of other people. It is thought to be the best and most civilized form of conduct that is acceptable in any situation and best suited to quality learning.

When students exhibit behavior that is low levels Marshall is asking them determine the degree of behavior they're displaying. If they can't Marshall then will ask them to determine the level of behavior that will benefit the class instead of hindering the progress of the class. He says that these easy methods almost always prompt students to behave in a way that is appropriate.

Superior Venues feature procedures that facilitate learning

Harry Wong and Rosemary Wong (2009) recommend that teachers adopt procedures that allow their classes to run as well-oiled machinery. The Wongs', many years the most sought-after educational consultants around the globe advise that if you want your class to run efficiently, you should teach your students the proper procedures for each class activity, and then let students practice these techniques until they understand them on their own.

There are numerous methods involved in teaching and learning However, don't let this discourage you. A majority of Wongs recommendations are available in the Internet. The following book would be highly recommended you to read: "Harry K. Wong and the Meaning of the Classroom Management"

Written by Linda Star (2006). Browser: 'Linda Star 2006 Wong Management.'

Superior Venues minimize factors that can hinder learning

These are brief descriptions of the main obstacles to learning in schools and ways you can tackle them.

> Information/Brain Incompatibility. Instruction is not appropriate to the students' cognitive abilities. Solution: Make sure that your teaching methods, information that you impart are compatible or compatible with students' abilities at various levels that develop the brain.

Informational Overload. A lot of information is offered in the lessons given. Solution: We've seen that the brain has trouble in processing a variety of issues in a short time. Students should only have one or two things to be thinking about during every lesson, and they should revisit them frequently.

> Physical or Mental Fatigue. It is a common reason why people feel fatigue.

> Resolution: Avoid fatigue by changing your activities regularly and interspersing them with time of discussion, listening or observing, reading and contemplation in silence.

• Physical discomfort. Physical discomfort is a major obstacle to learning. Solution: Avoid any element in the class that causes students to feel uncomfortable, like temperatures that are too high or low or noises, insufficient lighting or seating or sitting in a seated position for too long without moving.

> Psychosocial Discomfort. Fear anxiety, fear, and dread inhibit students from learning. Resolution: Ensure that you encourage a feeling of safety and acceptance, personal security of inclusion, and camaraderie.

- Instructional Inefficiency. Learning slows down when students aren't active. Solution: Plan each class or day to make an effective use of your time with engaging educational activities that students are interested in.

Unsuitable Levels of Complexity. When learning tasks are too challenging or easy, students can learn little. Resolution: Make lessons challenging enough that, with some effort, students can progress with ease. Introduce new learning in conjunction with the existing knowledge of students However, it should be within reach, and just ahead of their current standards of learning.

- Lack of relevance. Students frequently find it difficult to be involved in educational activities that do not have a connection with their personal or professional lives. Solution: Engage students in activities that are connected to their lives or specific interest. If students are required to research obscure topics, supplement your teaching with images or anecdotes, physical demonstrations and puzzles, as well as challenges and other activities that draw attention.

Attention to Needs of Students. In order for learning to take place correctly the psychosocial needs of students should be addressed. As we've noted the most common need include safety, feeling of belonging, joy and success, a sense of purpose, and a sense of being competent. Resolution: Make sure you are ensuring that students' physical, psychological and educational requirements are being met regularly. Discuss this issue with your students.

Four Jewels of Facet, High-Quality Learning Venues

They provide for the physical, social and intellectual needs

They create a climate of enthusiasm, positivity and optimism

They promote and encourage the importance of civil and responsible behavior.

They reflect an atmosphere of safety, efficiency, and camaraderie

Chapter 7: Planning And Management

Learning Venues

Warm-up Quiz

Select the suitable option to complete each section.

1. "Class Venue" is "classroom" as an) syllabus and (b) the physical as well as emotional environments and c) ethnic makeup for students and d) lighting design

2. The most crucial considerations in the venues is A) the needs of students as well as) design and third) an accomodation that is comfortable, and d) breaks for food

3. A renowned authority who has long ago defined the traits of students at different stages of their intellectual development such as: the following:) Glasser, b) Piaget and 3.) Marshall, d) Ginott

4. Who is the ultimate accountable for the organization of the venue for instruction: a) students and b) custodians, c) teacher and the d) the curriculum committee

5. This was not considered as an important factor in the classroom The following were not mentioned as important considerations: the) emotional tone and b) student movement and c) teacher station and d) fatigue monitors

6. The TONE of the learning environment is a reference to one of the following factors: A) inadequate expectations (a) unmet expectations, the absence of expectations,) instructors in charge (c) well-mannered students, and d) the atmosphere of emotion

7. A major authority of today for civility in the classroom: A) Mohandas Gandhi, b) Helen Keller, c) Ralph Tyler, d) P. M. Forni

8. A very strong advocate for a condition of the venue by Marvin Marshall: a) positive attitude as well as) orderliness,) co-operation and the third) parental involvement

9. A renowned authority on how teachers, in the first instance of meeting students, could leave an impressive impression by using 1.) Piaget, b) Tyler, the third) Gandhi, d) Linsin

10. A person of authority who advised instructors to increase the influence of their pupils by offering students choices to choose from: (a) Wong; b) Tyler and c) Marshall; d) Piaget

10-Point Summary

Choose the top 10 assertions or suggestions that are highlighted within this Facet. Discuss them and put the 10 most important contentions in order of their impact.

Terms Selection and Review

Choose and explain using your own words, 7 concepts within this Facet that resonate strongly with you. Sort them in order and describe the meanings behind them.

Seven Key Implications for Teaching

Within this Facet Choose and then briefly explain 1) what you think the overall to be the seven most important aspects for teaching, and) how you intend to incorporate these seven aspects in your overall teaching method.

One-Page Concept Map

Draw a sketch of the contents of this Facet on a single sheet of paper. Draw the interconnections. Create a memorable presentation. (For assistance with the process of graphic mapping, simply type "concept mapping' in the search bar of your Internet web browser.)

Try it out, using your Concept Map

Try to explain yourself in simple terms the purpose importance, value, and interrelationships of the elements included within your map. Modify the map if needed for better efficiency or clarity. After that you can save your map for future reference and go over it.

END OF FACET 4 - PLEASE PROCEED TO FACET 5

Facet 5 - connect personally with all your Students

Your goal is to develop and apply the principles and processes that create quality relationships both personal and professional with all your students.

Your Principal Duties

Your teaching effectiveness is contingent on your ability to build relationships with students that are personal to them. Although you might not be able to make connections with every one of them however, you are sure to connect with the majority and the stronger these connections are the better your students perform in school. Here are three tips for taking steps in this direction.

First, you must recognize the needs of your students at the grade you teach.

The second is to ensure that you are meeting those requirements in the manner that is feasible.

3. Determine always to engage with your students with a manner that is friendly open, honest, positive and respectful.

In truth, that's the only thing you have to accomplish to make enough personal connections. You must involve every student in that initiative, and remain within the confines of schooling and professionalism.

What experts say

Through the years many highly respected experts have advised teachers to build strong professional and personal connections between them and their learners. The most important characteristics of suggested connections are respect, kindness and encouragement. The process of creating the connections is quite easy. Here are some suggestions:

- Display a positive, useful Teacher
- Understand the pitfalls of students and meet their needs
> Maintain effective Class Communication
- Create a atmosphere of optimism and positivity
- Involve your students in ensuring that they maintain Civil, Responsible behavior.

It's your responsibility to start these efforts, and it is your responsibility as well as your students to assume responsibility for adhering to and adhering to these rules. Take the necessary steps to create that shared obligation. Here are some ideas for doing that, starting with your teacher persona.

Connecting with Students via Your Teacher's Persona

As was mentioned previously, nearly all students are at ease with teachers with attractive personalities that can be created and easily projected.

You'll be able to remember the charismatic aspect of your personality as a teacher is a mix of attributes and actions that attract students and motivate students to work with your. Particularly effective is your attention to detail, your cheerful attitude, a smile that is ready with a sense of humor, enthusiasm, optimism, evident competence, willingness to aid and communicate effectively and surprise students, and a genuine pleasure teaching students.

It is possible to show other characteristics, for example, your love of teaching, your unique skills, your experience, traveling, your early work experience and other passions like cooking or cooking, poetry, music, art acting, and more. When interacting with students, make sure to avoid self-aggrandizement--but do mention an interesting tidbit about yourself now and then.

Connecting with students through their Characteristics

We now turn our attention to observations regarding students' development behaviors that offer insights into the behavior and preferences of students in different levels of development. The first step is to discuss remarks and suggestions from experts on the behavior of school age students.

>> Jean Piaget (1951), an internationally renowned Swiss development psychologist, who was mentioned earlier in the article, offered a wealth of useful details on how children grow intellectually and behave emotionally and behaviorally in their school years. To make it easier for you I've included the brief outline of his findings:

Concerning students in the Primary Grades (Ages 5-8). In this stage of their lives children are extremely active and are very open to learning. They are incredibly affectionate, love music, stories and rhythmic exercises as well as an incredible ability to master languages. They aren't a fan of sitting in a solitary position for long. They aren't able to distinguish between play and work. Their primary needs are activities, stimulation, attention to and interaction with adults and other students, as well as often rest.

Socially, they are learning to play with each other. They love affection and attention from others and enjoy music as well as art, rhythms stories, and other activities which involve animals.

For students In Intermediate Grades (Ages 9-11). When students enter the school year 4 and begin to become more able to be independent, however, they will still require love and attention from their teachers. Their love for wildlife and the natural world is not going away. Socially, they would like to be able to enjoy their time with each other. The behavior of their individual members begins to follow the norms of their peers. They realize the need for rules and rules enforcement for games as well as in class behaviour. In their speech, they are more likely to be more argumentative. Some are vocal and loudly assertive, but are now beginning to believe in reasoning when trying to convince other people. Teachers' authority is no longer to be taken for granted. Students are sometimes able to argue with the teacher, argue about it, or even be rude.

Regarding middle school grades (Ages 12-14). At this point, students' behaviour becomes more unpredictable and teachers must have specialized skills and knowledge when it comes to teaching and establishing relationships with their students. Students are starting to explore the limits of customs and rules. Their fascination with teachers has diminished, but it is being replaced by reverence and love towards teachers that are fascinating and attentive, well-informed and understanding. They are also helpful.

Concerning secondary school grades (Ages 15-18). Students who enter secondary school are quickly becoming more adept at thinking. They have a tendency for thinking about theories and are able to identify reasons, motives and the places in which everything happens. They are thinking about the possible as well as the real and have developed a strong desire to find the right way over the wrong. Their reasoning ability reflects the optimism that is typical of adolescents. Propositional thinking is a recurring theme: "If I do so and so, then and so will happen." Interest in individuals as well as society at large is increasing rapidly.

For these students, a lot of society's laws and rules seem insignificant or irrelevant, so breaking them isn't anymore considered to be absolutely untrue. They are unable to comprehend the reasons why anything isn't perfect--politics and institutions, human relationships and so on. They are with a negative view of how institutions and people function. They might be scathing about adult social norms and practices however, for the most portion of their actions, their conduct is fairly well with the social rules.

As they get closer to the end of secondary school the students start to relax emotionally. They are more aware of themselves and have become more comfortable with their bodies and their feelings and are beginning consider what they would like to accomplish in the near future. Teachers are able to interact with students as adults as students go to their favourite teachers as role models.

Engaging students via their Needs

The needs of students in this context are related to a general sense of emotional, physical and psychosocial well-being. These needs, which are also that of teachers, comprise the physical requirements for nutrition as well as comfort and periods of rest and activity; emotional needs for security and security, pleasure, as well as support and psychosocial requirements for attention to oneself to be accepted, a sense of belonging, acceptance other students, feeling of belonging, and a sense of accomplishment. If you are able to help your students meet these demands, the better they'll focus and be able to learn.

Note: You should ensure that your students know that you are aware of their requirements and try to ensure that they are taken care of. However students must be aware that there are professional requirements which students have to help you meet. The first need is that students make an effort to be a good learner as well as to be cooperative with you and with one another as well as for students to behave with respect and dignity. When you first meet with your class discuss these requirements and the ways yourself and the children will be able to meet these needs. It is likely that you will need to reiterate these concepts at times.

\>\> Matthew Lieberman (in Cook, 2013) states that our desire to be connected with others is as essential as our need to eat and water. He cites studies that show that all mammals including rodents and humans, suffer tremendously when their social connections are damaged. Consider answering this question yourself What do you consider this need to connect means for teachers, students and classrooms?

\>\> Abraham Maslow (1943), an early leading psychologist was among the first to emphasize that people of all ages are prone to needs that, if not fulfilled, cause feelings of anxiety, frustration and uncertainty. These issues hinder self-confidence and enterprise. In his 1943 work, "A Theory of Human Motivation" Maslow hypothesized seven clusters of needs that came into the equation for everyone. Maslow presented these clusters as organized in the form of an arc which places the essential needs at the bottom, and higher priority needs closer to the top. To view a range of ways that Maslow's hierarchy is illustrated, search for 'Maslow's hierarchy in your browser. Many illustrations from his hierarchy will be displayed that show the following order from the bottom to the top in this order:

The necessity to ensure Physiological well-being. Nutrition is the most important element sufficient rest and movement according to the need; adequate temperatures and light; and ease.

The need for safety. The second most important - the general sense of security and absence of any social or physical threat or danger.

The need to belong. To be a part of and to feel accepted at school and the teacher(s) and classmates.

The need for confidence. Respect for oneself, respect from others, and a reputation as being smart and skilled and regarded as an honest person.

Need for Competence. To improve your knowledge and able to clearly articulate and complete the duties of one's job; and to be a great communicater.

The need for aesthetics. Being aware of being aware of, grateful for and connected to beauty in its various types.

Need to be Self-Actualized. To be the best person you could be, you must be proficient, understanding capable, self-directed and respectful of other people.

Maslow claimed that both of his learners (and we) perform best when the above requirements are met and not so well when one of them are not.

\>\> William Glasser (2001), a well-known psychiatrist who was extremely interested in education, stressed the importance of addressing the needs of students. He highlighted five essential needs of school that must be fulfilled in order for the majority of students to be successful at the classroom:

~ Safety. To feel safe, secure and free of physical or emotional danger

Feeling of belonging. To be loved by classmates and teachers

~ Power. Participation in the group and to have an input in group decision-making

~ Fun. To enjoy a happy interaction with other students in class activities

~ Freedom. to make personal decisions for oneself

Glasser advised teachers to realize that almost all students are able to achieve success in school, given the right environment and guidance. In order to ensure success teachers must make use of influence rather than coercion to help students with their learning. The types of influence that teachers can use Glasser recommended include encouraging, listening, appreciation trust, respect, and appreciation.

>> Richard Sagor (2003), an academician, researcher and writer, utilizes the term 'CBUPOs' in order to assist teachers in understanding and address students' needs at school. Sagor's descriptions of student needs differ than those used by Glasser. Sagor's criteria are: Competence, Belonging and Usefulness. notes and the summarising

y and optimism (hence it being the CBUPO abbreviation).

Sagor says that students tend to keep positive memories (which can strengthen CBUPOs) CBUPOs) as happy pictures which reside in their brains and that they constantly try to recreate to relive that "happy feeling. It is possible to access Sagor's fascinating theories by entering into your browser : 'Sagor CBUPO theories.'

You Author. This is for your consideration. your Author's more extensive list of the needs of students along with a discussion of the roles of teachers in meeting these needs.

The need for safety and security. It is accomplished by reducing schools and classrooms, the personal risk and a sense of emotional or physical risk.

The need for interaction with other students. It is met by providing regular programs and activities that allow students can play, interact with others, talk about, and collaborate.

The need to feel a sense belonging. It is addressed by helping students recognize that they have a valid identity, role and value in the schools and within groups as well as by offering opportunities for all students to take part in significant ways.

A need for a feeling of optimism. This is met by continuous evidence and assurance that every student has the ability to be successful in their learning and to be successful in school and be supported in achieving this.

The need to feel a sense personal dignity. This is achieved by ensuring that children are treated respectfully in all situations and by teaching students the reasons and appropriate actions to treat others with respect.

A need for a sense of personal power. This is achieved by regularly involving students in making decisions and choices during classes.

The need for pleasure. This is achieved by ensuring that students feel happy or satisfied during school and in class.

Need to be competent. This is accomplished by helping students create evidence of how they are becoming ever more proficient, skilled and productive.

If the above needs are being met students tend to feel satisfied and optimistic. They also feel co-operative. If one or more the needs are not fulfilled, students are likely to feel uneasy, disengaged or unappreciated. They may also feel anxious, frightened, or perhaps unsatisfied All of which can affect learning.

Connecting with Students through Communication

Communication plays an integral part in teachers' efforts to engage with their students and promote learning. Students tend to be the most happy and can do the best things when they are they are given the opportunity to interact with other students in person. They're also more likely to be successful in their learning when they can effectively communicate and with teachers. Through the years several well-known experts have offered suggestions on how teachers can better communicate with their students. Here are a few ideas:

>> William Glasser (2001) urged teachers to interact with their students, treating them as equals. There should be no shaming or

preaching, moralizing, making them feel guilty, or making promises. When problems arise it is suggested that teachers explain the situation, specify the steps to take and then ask students to assist in resolving the issue.

> Richard Milner (2011) says teachers can communicate the best by keeping in mind the positive value, merit, as well as potential of all students.

>> Stephen Covey (2004) emphasizes that we communicate more effectively if we strive first to comprehend another person (in this case, our students) before trying to help them comprehend us.

>> Fred Jones (2007) emphasizes the communication potential of body language, calling it one of the teachers' most valuable assets. It's frequently more efficient than the use of verbal communication. Body language's primary components include eyes, body contact body carriage, voice tone and facial expressions all of which convey excitement, seriousness, pleasure and displeasure. Are you able to think of instances of the teacher's body language which inhibits communication?

>> Marvin Marshall (2016) has been for a long time one of the greatest advocates for ensuring positive and optimistic classrooms. MarvinMarshall.com provides the Internet

website for his Discipline without Stress (2016) which Marshall encourages teachers to incorporate optimism, positive thinking and behavior choices in all interactions with their students. Particularly, he counsels teachers to regularly consider, "How can I react or act or speak about this in a positive manner?" And he further recommends that teachers offer students opportunities to choose their own path, arguing that students tend to prefer options than to a set of instructions.

>> Haim Ginott (1972) believed that effective communication is particularly effective in maintaining a warm personal tone within the classroom. He often stressed that teaching is incredibly personal for students who want to be listened to by teachers and are extremely sensitive to the words teachers speak to them, and how they speak to them. He advised teachers to stress the following. Take note of the language Ginott used and try to imagine a classroom scenario where you can implement his ideas:

• Congruous communication. Communication that is consistent with the students' opinions about the situation and about their own feelings about the situation. Example (in reaction to mistakes and mistakes) teacher says, "We all make mistakes. They're part of learning and can teach us a lot. In the present how do you feel we can do?"

~ Sane messages. Use the opportunity to address situations, rather than their past behavior or character. For instance, instead of scolding students with the words "You are too loud or unconsiderate or poor citizens,"" address the consequences you're experiencing by telling them "I believe that the noise level is too loud to be conducive to learning. Are you able to assist us?"

~ Conferring dignity. When teachers treat their students as equals without sermons, moralizing, inflicting guilt or making commitments. For instance, if a change in behavior is required, it is possible to declare, "I have a couple of suggestions you could consider trying. Here's a list of them . . . Which one do you think would be the most effective?"

• Inviting students to cooperate. When a problem arises, you outline the issue, outline what you need to do and ask students' involvement in solving the issue. Example: A teacher says, "I believe this discussion has become out of control. What are we able to do to get back to a normal pace?"

Avoiding questions about why (why did you do this or this?). Most often, they make students feel guilty and defensive. Instead, you could tell them, "Here's what needs to be done ..." or "What do you think we should do?"

Inflicting sanctions on the use of sarcasm or punishment. Inform students that sarcasm or verbal abuse can be harmful. They do not make others feel like you or desire to be better. Instead, they're likely to be a source of anger or an urge to take revenge.

In the end, here Ginott's most memorable advice about interacting to students (1972, 13). 13.); "As a teacher I've reached the terrifying realization that I'm the most important component of the school. It is my personal attitude that determines the atmosphere. It is my mood that affects the weather. As a teacher, I hold the ability to create the (student's) life difficult or joyful. I can be a weapon to torture or an instrument of inspiratoin. I am able to humiliate or laugh and heal or hurt. In all instances, it's my choice of response as to whether the situation can be de-escalated or escalated as well as (a student) is dehumanized or humanized".

>> P. M. Forni (2006) A leading expert on encouraging good behavior in schools Explains that both civil conduct and civil communication convey a tone of hope, optimism kindness, courtesy respect, good manners, and generosity. The author argues that teachers

who demonstrate these qualities and encourage students to do exactly the same are widely appreciated and are often praised. He states that one of the most important ways teachers can help students is to assist them to demonstrate civility in all interactions with other people. Civility is defined as having respect for other people and their opinions through the use of kindness, courtesy, good manners as well as sincerity and compassion.

>> C. M. Charles (2000) identified a variety of teacher initiatives to improve communication and foster connections between and between students. Here are some examples:

Ethics and Moral Behavior. Learn from your students how to show the same qualities in their interactions with other people, a sense of compassion, honesty, respect fairness, and kindness.

Effective Communication. Discuss with your students about three to four items they could use to create a positive effects on others--e.g. Smile, pay attention, repeat what someone else says Ask if they've had the pleasure of hearing about (name an individual or something that could be unfamiliar to another person).

• Personal respect. Offer practice sessions where students acknowledge each other politely take note of the opinions of others and maintain a calm manner when their opinions are in dispute.

Positive outlook. Students should be able to project positive personalities and positivity, as well as humor and excitement.

> Colorin Colorado (a website, not a person). If you have students who speak Spanish or are just starting to learn English or are just beginning to learn English, you'll find this site extremely useful when trying to communicate with your students. Particularly recommended are two articles available on the Internet accessible. The first is 'Getting To Know Your ELLs: Six Steps to success' Written by Lydia Breiseth (2013), and the other is an article written by the staff of the university in 2007 entitled "How to Create a Friendly Classroom Environment. To get access to the articles, just type in "Colorin Colorado" into your browser. The articles that you find are useful for teaching students from different backgrounds. They offer ideas for:

Building connections with students of communities whose family traditions and values are different from those of the dominant Helping students deal with the feelings of anger, home-sickness, hostility, frustration or resentment that they might feel towards the new environment.

Helping students gradually to accept and accept their new surroundings and cultural norms

You can better understand your students in relation to their body language, actions drawing, behavior, and other behaviors

Icebreakers and getting to know-you-me activities that students like

There are many questions you can ask that will prompt responses for example, questions about pets and sports, weekends and social occasions

Instilling trust through paying attention as well as responding with a manner students feel comfortable

A Few Other Observations

Perhaps you're exhausted from what you've seen within this Facet and may need a little piece of assurance that your efforts really worthwhile. Here are some expert's comments on teaching that you may be reassured by:

• Shaun Killian on What Makes Great Teachers. According to his Internet article titled 'What Makes an Excellent teacher' (accessed 2017) Killian states that there is no doubt that teachers can have an effective, positive influence that has a major impact in the performance of students in school, however, often, due to various reasons there are many teachers who don't do this. Killian lists several characteristics that can be seen as exceptional teachers, such as a love to teach, the highest expectations for students, ability to instruct and dedication. He also points to the evidence presented from Barber as well as Mourshed (2007) that found that "students placed with teachers who perform better generally learn three times as fast students who are placed with less-performing teachers".

>> Syed Meer (2016) published The Top 7 Qualities and Characteristics of a successful teacher. (https://owlcation.com/academia/Characteristics-Of-A-Good-Teacher). Meer acknowledges that every teacher wants to excel at their jobs, but the majority of them do not demonstrate the experience and skills that make them this. Meer offers this list of the qualities he believes constitutes the most desirable teacher qualities Congeniality and friendliness thorough knowledge of the subject that is to be covered, a charming personality, excellent communications skills and a a good sense of humor.

For more authoritative information regarding high-quality teachers and effective techniques for teaching, refer to the following Internet content.

> Baker, J., and Emerson, L. (2014). Reciprocal Teaching: Seeming is believing. The following is

an interesting article about the benefits of Reciprocal Teaching (research proved) which significantly improves students' comprehension of the text reading.

> Briggs, S. (2015). 12 Things Students Recall Most About Teachers who are good. This article is for older students, however its fundamental concepts are applicable to all students.

> Gard, L. (2014). What students remember most about Teachers. For students in the early years however, it is relevant to all age groups.

> Gallagher, E. (2013). The effects of teacher-student relationships The Academic and Social outcomes of low-income Middle and high school students. OPUS.

> Hare, J. (2016). Survey reveals what students really think of teachers. This article concisely outlines an extensive survey that is focused on the things students think about their teachers, both positive and negative.

> Labaree, D. (2000). On the nature of teaching as well as Teacher Education. Complex practices that appear easy. This is among the few articles in the field of scholarly research that are both educational and entertaining to read. Worthwhile. A good topic for discussion groups regarding teaching.

> Provenzano, N. (2014). Three Ways to Create meaningful connections with your students.

This is an interesting and detailed personal account of teacher in the classroom.

> Rimm-Kaufman S. and Sandilos, L. (2016.) Enhancing Students' Relationships with Teachers to provide essential support for Learning. It includes descriptions of positive qualities in teachers which encourage connections, and the negative qualities of teachers that hinder learning. It is an excellent discussion of teacher-student interactions as well as how they form and how they can enhance learning.

> Zakrzewski, V. (2012). Four ways teachers can show They Are Dedicated.

Now, a Few Important A few words on irresponsible teacher behavior

The suggestions contained within this Guidebook are intended to assist you to teach more effectively, respectfully and in a responsible manner. To be honest, most of us often fall short of these standards. Here are some examples of teachers' errors that are reckless since they fail to take into consideration the wellbeing of students. There's no need to provide explanations since you already understand what they mean.

- Inadequate preparation
> Insensitivity to student characteristics and their needs

A lack of understanding of the conditions under which students are most successful in learning
- Inability or inability to effectively communicate with students
> Trying to influence students through demands and coercion
- Failure to use the most efficient teaching methods

More thoughts on developing and presenting a quality persona

We've often stressed how important it is to have a "Teacher Persona', referring to this as being the professional character that teachers exhibit when working with students. It is actually an enhancement of the personality of the teacher and may include enhancements in some of the most important areas like charisma as well as positive interactions, communication and sensitivity to the students' demands, and a mix of incredibly efficient techniques and methods of teaching. Here are some additional ideas you may find useful.

In order to establish a good relationship with your class, start with a pleasant and attentive way to remember and learn names of students, thank each one individually, and show respect for any concerns they may have (with some useful tips or observations) Ask students what they find most enjoyable in their school and with teachers, and state what you will be teaching in a manner that students will find enjoyable and effective. While you are doing this, make sure that you can follow up your suggestions with useful actions. Engage students in a personal way and encourage their cooperation. be attentive to their needs, speak clearly and provide assistance and other useful direction.

When you first make contact with students who are new to your class, you should clarify the goals of the class (stated as aspirations, possibilities and outcomes of high quality) Also, describe your overall way of teaching (organized and exciting, attractive, fun and helpful, with reasonable suggestions, but not a lot of bossing or judging) and demonstrate the ways you'll employ techniques that students find fun and beneficial, such as "reciprocal teaching" and "conceptual change', both of which are being reviewed in the near future.

Include also the ways you'll create a positive atmosphere in the classroom, with positive and friendly and provide feedback and guidance to keep everyone on the right track having fun and moving forward. These efforts are crucial to the creation of of mutual respect and confidence between your students and yourself that in turn enhance collaboration, efficiency and overall performance.

A note of caution: Though an effective teacher persona is fairly easy to create however, it can be fragile. Sometimes , it is damaged by just a single word or facial gesture. Therefore, make sure to remove from your interaction style all attitude, rudeness, sarcasm, remarks, negative criticism as well as jokes and remarks that may cause offence to. They can be very damaging against your students and you. Additionally, your inability to clearly communicate what you plan to impart and your inattention to your students as well as your demands that students think are unreasonable, a chaotic presentation, and the inability to keep your the promises you make.

Chapter 8: How To Work And Connect With Students

Warm-up Quiz

Select the appropriate option for each section.

1. Your teaching personality is A) your inherent personality and the second) your teaching style and the third) your personality change as well as D) your demonstrated personality

2. A renowned authority on students' requirements in school The following are the names of his authority: a) Glasser; b) Martindale and the third) Chamberlin; d) Carnegie

3. A renowned authority on the development of civility is: A) Piaget; b) Forni; C) Hunter; d) Dewey

4. The word "civility" is closest to the notion of: a) accountability as well as) authenticity as well as C) enthusiasm; and d) respect for others.

5. In this Facet and other Facets the persona of your teacher is described as being an: A) malleable or it is) static or static; in c) the same as your social persona as well as the third) generally positive

6. The primary characteristic of the "connections" that are portrayed by this Facet is the following: A) dynamic and dynamic, and)

emotional and emotional, c) conjectural or a) existence-based

7. Positive teacher-student relationships can be developed through A) the tradition or a) nature and the c) communication, and d) parental intervention

8. Which of the following figures helped the most in fostering connections between students and teachers? a) Tyler, b) Dewey, c) Skinner, d) Ginott

9. Who advised us to learn to read others' minds before trying to understand them (a.) Covey, b) Glasser and (c) Marshall, d) Linsin

10. Which of the following advocated for using the body language of a student to affect students' behavior? A) Piaget and B) Covey, c) Forni, and d) Jones

10-Point Summary

Determine what you consider to be the top 10 important arguments presented in this Facet and place these in order according to their importance and explain each one in your own phrases.

Terms Selection and Review

Pick and define using your own words the 10 concepts discussed on the Facet which resonates with you the most. Put them in order of importance, and then justify your selections.

Seven Implications of Teaching

From the information contained in this Facet Select and concisely explain:

1. What do you consider to be the seven most significant implications for teaching
2. What will you do to emphasize these seven points in your teaching method?

One-Page Concept Map

Draw a conceptual diagram of the contents of this Facet on one page of paper. Mark connections. Create a memorable presentation. (For help , type in "concept mapping" into your browser)

Make Practice using Your Concept Map

Try to explain using your own language, the characteristics of the interrelationships, their value, and of the elements included on your conceptual map. Restructure the map if needed to improve clarity or flow. Then, save your conceptual map for future reference and for review.

Self-Assessment Exercise

There are two types of qualities that students admire from their teachers. One is personal , and the other is professional. Both overlap significantly. Assess yourself objectively about your capacity to communicate these traits effectively. Select three qualities in each area you're good at and three areas in which areas that you may need to work on:

> My Personal Traits. Attractive, enjoyable, and flexible; tolerant; trustworthy steady; unwavering; personality; fun; positive disposition; interesting particular interests and talents.

> My Professional Traits. Very helpful, friendly and competent, reliable and honest; a great communicator; is able to understand students and adept in teaching; persistent committed; makes learning enjoyable or even fun good organizer; great explanation; innovative concepts.

The creation of a Teaching Persona who connects with students

Discuss how you can show these qualities in the way you teach. Discuss with your professional study partners:

Personal Characteristics. Positivity and optimism (upbeat and positive, able to do) sincere (genuine) and friendly (open, friendly) reliable (can be relied on) and pleasant (smiling smile, positive side) fun (entertaining intelligent) and attentive (listens to what you say, makes eye contact) with a the ability to be funny (controlled).

• Instructional Skills. Knowledgable (know what you're talking about) Prepared (ready to teach and interact) clear (express what you intend to say) Clarity of presentation (understandable)

and reasonable (persuasive well-balanced) and adept at leading (motivational clear direction with helpful feedback) Good in explaining (clear concise, clear, and understandable) and persistent (don't abandon the cause) and help students improve on their mistakes (uplifting and positive advice rather than demeaning comments).

> First meeting with students and self-introduction. Smile (genuinely) smile, express delight to be with students, repeat and remember names, write down the positive qualities of every student, write about you personal experiences (briefly) with family members, pets and hobbies, as well as interests and particular abilities (e.g. poetry, music or magic or acting) or travels (places photographs, places souvenirs, objects).

END OF FACET 5 INPUT - PLEASE PROCEED TO FACET 6

Facet 6 - You Utilize the scientific research to teach

Your Goal: To comprehend and implement instructional methods that are scientifically proven to increase the quality of learning for students.

Your Prime Duties

As a Professional Teacher, you must choose to learn about the use of methods of instruction that have been proven to foster a strong learning. In other Facets we will make note of the contributions of John Hattie in Australia and Robert Marzano in the United States the most renowned translators of research for the field of high-quality teaching.

In a manner that they are independent of one another, Hattie and Marzano have identified the impact on learning from around 350 instructional strategies. To be fair to those two experts, we will take note of their most important findings, particularly the conditions for teaching and strategies that encourage exceptional learning students of various levels.

Each of Hattie as well as Marzano have also discovered an extensive number of well-known methods of teaching that are not effective for promoting learning and therefore are is not worthy of your attention. In this article, we will look at a few of them however for the main part, we'll look at strategies that are extremely effective in helping students learn. In addition, you'll learn how you can integrate them into your method of teaching.

Marzano and Hattie's contributions in a Nutshell

In the last two decades John Hattie in Australia and Robert Marzano in the United States have independently examined huge amounts of research on teaching. Through their efforts, they have identified a set of teaching strategies that have been proven to promote exceptionally high rates of student learning. Marzano is currently proving his findings through in-school research that confirms and clarifies his findings.

When this article was writing in 2020, Hattie was director of the Melbourne Educational Research Institute at the University of Melbourne, Australia as well as Marzano was the head of the Marzano Research Laboratory in Centennial, Colorado, USA. Marzano and Hattie's work is alike and complementary, which gives more credibility to their independent conclusion.

It is evident that the word "interventions" refers to teacher-led conditions and actions they perform when instructing students in their learning.

In this facet the Author will draw the attention of a set which are the most efficient interventions. Some of them may be familiar to you. Others might not. If you follow the recommendations and engage your students in a way that is appropriate You will most likely witness significant improvement in the level of education your students receive. Thanks for these outstanding contributions we once more tip our high towards John Hattie and Robert Marzano for their efforts, which we will shortly review.

Let's first look at the characteristics of Hattie's as well as Marzano's research, and the conclusions they've drawn in a way that is independent of each other. This research may initially seem complicated. However, once you are able to get your head around it, you'll realize it to be logical, quite simple to comprehend and extremely valuable.

Her Major Efforts with Hattie

John Hattie has gone to the greatest lengths to determine and quantify the effectiveness of different conditions and methods teachers employ to help their students develop. He has studied data from over 300 million schoolchildren around the world He has identified a huge amount educators' particular instructional interventions (conditions and actions) and measured the effect each one of them appears to have on student learning. While a few unanswered concerns remain to be answered, her work has contributed to teaching in a remarkable way.

In the past, Hattie analyzed the data through a process known as meta-analysis. It pools the results of large amounts of research studies on a specific area and then analyzes the results as a whole. This method significantly increased the validity of the conclusions derived.

Recently, Hattie moved beyond meta-analysis to meta-meta-analysis, an approach which combines data from several existing meta-analyses. The process results in higher levels of confidence in findings drawn.

Through these researches, Hattie has discovered that a variety of well-known methods of teaching can actually encourage extraordinary learning, with some reaching extremely high levels. He has also discovered that many of the familiar methods that have been used for a long time yield only average learning while others are found to have no value. In this article, we will look at examples of these results.

Marzano's Major Efforts

Robert Marzano has also analyzed current research on teaching and has brought attention to various methods that teachers commonly make use of. His work has included;

> Pooling research data from vast quantities of current research

- Analyzing the data in a way that provides extremely accurate conclusions

The importance of identifying the results of specific practices in helping students learn

- Involving teachers in the implementation of the instructional techniques in controlled classrooms, and thereby being able to determine more precisely the extent to which they actually enhance learning

> expressing his findings in a language that practitioners quickly comprehend and utilize.

Similar to Hattie, Marzano has found that some of the well-known teaching methods are highly efficient in helping students learn, and others are ineffective or are not very effective. Additionally, he has focused specifically on the top-performing interventions, and has identified the effectiveness of each in helping students learn and has helped teachers use them effectively in their interactions with students.

Presently, Marzano continues to refine his most promising strategies through controlled research that have teachers from various schools, with his guidance they are applying the methods again and re-evaluating the results they have on students. Marzano has drawn his most recent conclusions from these well-managed studies, and his methods are extensively observed. The author has published his research findings and recommendations in numerous books, and offers seminars for educators and experts to assist teachers in learning to utilize the information in schools.

Selections of Hattie's and Marczano's Effect Estimates

We are now entering the unknown territory. Keep going and it will eventually become clear.

To determine the relative impact of different instructional techniques (meaning the extent to which each one aids in education), Hattie and Marzano both employ a method of statistical analysis invented by the statistician Jacob Cohen. The method produces what Cohen calls d-scores. They are the effects certain factors are likely to be able to have on achieving certain outcomes. In our instance we are particularly focused on factors that are proven to ensure high levels of education in the school setting that are not only average in learning, but also learning beyond the norm.

Hattie in her reports use Cohen's word "d-score" in order to describe the effectiveness of various instructional interventions.

Marzano uses Cohen's method, too, however he prefers "ES" (effect measurement) rather than the term 'd' when he writes his reports.

"ES" and "d-value" are terms that are interchangeable. They are the same.

In the coming discussions, we will be focusing on several instructional strategies which consistently produce high D-scores (high ES) meaning they have been tested and proven to result in extraordinary increase in learning. Cohen offered the following benchmarks for understanding D-effects. These are decimal percents that measure one or more standards deviations student growth in their learning, which can be as little as in one term, but often over the course of a year. Cohen suggests:

D = .8 A growth by eight-tenths one standard deviation. Very strong

d = .5 A growth of one-half of a standard deviation. This is an average effect

d = .2 A growth of two-tenths of a standard deviation. A small impact

Hattie discovered that the average D-score (effect size) in the instructional interventions that he studied at d = .4 that is four tenths of a standard deviation in the growth of learning (usually over a single academic year) which is a bit lower than Cohen's theoretical average. In this way, Hattie suggests that we take the value of d = .4 as a typical students' growth in their learning (typically however, not necessarily within an academic calendar year).

Let's get to the gems The jewels: Both Hattie as well as Marzano have identified a significant variety of methods that result in D- scores, or ES, that are much higher than the threshold of .4 and even far above Cohen's "large effect" value that is d = .8. In this article, we will highlight some of their most effective methods and encourage you to integrate them into your method of teaching.

A short interlude to address a few ambiguous questions

We also noted the fact that John Hattie has quantified the individual effects on learning from more than 300 teacher interventions. He concluded that the personal results of the interventions varied from to 0.0 (no impact at all) all the way to the number of 1.57 (just four times the average size of effect and astonishly high). You may recall that he calculated that the d value of .4 (four-tenths of one standard deviation improvement in achievement for students) is the average of the student's learning gains over the course of one academic year.

These conclusions and findings while extremely useful as we strive to make improvements to teaching have a few unanswered questions for instance, could only one of these methods, out of the numerous that teachers frequently employ, encourage in itself a whole year's worth of improvement in the teaching in a specific classroom or grade level?

It's a bit absurd. If this is not the case, how can we determine the effects of multiple interventions incorporated throughout the year? If one specific intervention has the ability to do so, can't multiple proven interventions, when used together, result in significant higher levels of education? You might think this, but there is no evidence to prove to support this claim.

Some other issues have been raised also. To keep things in perspective I'll list the two main ones: In Hattie's study, there is no uniform description of how teachers organize or implement the various methods they employ within their classrooms. For instance feedback is an intervention that has been proven to exert a powerful influence on student learning. Teachers provide feedback in many different ways, and it is possible to imagine that these different approaches will result in different outcomes. This is the case to the vast majority of interventions Hattie has identified. The problem is that we don't have exact and standardized descriptions for what these interventions included or the way they were implemented.

A related issue is that it can be difficult, if it is not impossible, to pinpoint the impact of one impact in classrooms that are being influenced by many different methods and circumstances. (Marzano attempts to address this issue through his controlled research.)

In spite of these concerns there is a general consensus that both Marzano and Hattie's research will be of great help in improving learning and teaching. As time passes teachers who implement their ideas will definitely be able to see significant improvement in the learning of their students however the effects of the interventions featured could differ.

To lessen the uncertainty in the future, in this work we will concentrate (with the exception of a few essential exceptions) on interventions in teaching that have resulted in an effect size of at most d = .50 that is significantly above Hattie's typical of .40. With d = .50 defined as a threshold of acceptable, it's plausible to conclude that the strategies we be examining now actually increase the level of learning over the average.

Concerning the Top-Rated Teaching Interventions

The strategies for teaching that are ultimately suggested in this article are based on John Hattie's analysis of more than 350 Instructional

Factors, as well as from Robert Marzano's studies and tests of several highly effective Instructional factors (accessed in 2020).

All in all, these selections typically have D-scores (ES) in the range of .50 or higher, though certain choices from Marzano's research are less. Also, each of the elements we examine is either an action of the teacher directly or a specific requirement which teachers create to improve learning.

Your Author's Picks from Marzano's top-tier intervention elements

These powerful interventions to which we are now focusing our attention stem from a range of instructional programs discovered in the work of Marzano and Haystead in 2009. For more information, make use of your web browser to view the report titled "Meta-Analysis Haystead, M., and Marzano, R., August 2009'.

In the research, Haystead and Marzano indicate the ES of each intervention that they measured the effects of. The effect they measured for the interventions they examined were ES = .42 which is a little higher than what Hattie observed. Then, Haystead and Marzano also identified for each intervention the level of learning in percentiles which is attributable to the intervention. This is an important figure since "percentile" is a word that is familiar to all teachers.

Below is a selection of Marzano's most highly rated interventions, listed by effect size. Important to keep in mind that the interventions listed in the list above are for primarily instructional strategies and their effect sizes tend to be smaller than effects of non-instructional factors like teacher credibility or the teachers' personal perception of competence.

The seven elements chosen from a list offered from Haystead as well as Marzano (2009) were identified with the letter "M" to signify Marzano. Again, the following are the interpretations of your author. For the most up-to-date information, refer to the study of Haystead as well as Marzano (2009).

Haystead's and Marzano's eight Intervention Elements

M1. Teacher clearly explains the goals and Objectives that must be achieved. The top rank results in the growth in learning of 25 percentiles over an entire schooling year. This is well over the average.

M2. Teacher Uses Interactive Games. Students, supervised by the teacher participate in competitive learning games. Growth in learning of 20 percentile marks, which is over the average.

M3. Teachers Help Students Find Similarities and Distinctions. A common learning activity that encourages growth in learning by 20 percentile points significantly higher than normal.

M4.Teacher regularly engages students with Vocabulary Building. Teachers assist students in expanding their vocabulary, which results in an average growth in learning of 20 percentile points significantly higher than what is considered average.

M5.Teacher Demands Students to Write a Summary of What They've Learned. Students are asked to highlight clearly the key points in the lessons they've learned A growth in learning at 19 percentile, far above the average.

M6.Teacher Makes Use of Non-Linguistic Representations. Teachers use diagrams and physical movements during instruction. They then show students how to create diagrams, perform them physically, or show what they've learned. It yields an increase of 17 percentile points, which is well over average.

M7. Teacher Aids Students in Note-taking. Students are taught to note notes quickly and efficiently, getting a growth in their learning of

17 percentile points, which is well over the average.

Your Author's Choices from Hattie's top Intervention Elements

This article will review the 20 most notable instructional intervention components that were identified in the work of John Hattie, as reported by Shaun Killian. It is recommended that you read the complete list of interventions by Hattie and the corresponding d-values available on your web browser through Shaun Killian Shaun Killian - Hattie 2017, Evidence Based teaching.' (Note: Also look on for the Internet for the most recent publications of Hattie's latest research findings.) On the next list the word 'H" refers to Hattie as well as an indication of the impact the intervention is believed to possess in encouraging learning.

H1. The teacher engages students in Cognitive Task Analysis. Aids students to comprehend and visualize the things they want to understand. The effect has been verified to be over three times the normal rate of growth in understanding.

Conclusion

I hope that this book has been useful in helping you learn how to be a successful teacher assistant. The most important thing you must understand is that becoming a teacher assistant can be an extremely rewarding job, provided you're up to the task. There will be times you think you're not able to handle the workload anymore, and at those times, remind yourself the reason you chose to be a teacher assistant to begin with You must be motivated to take advantage of every opportunity to grow and grow.

Be aware that every student must receive respect, and dedication. They are just that children, and it is important to become extremely gentle with your children. There will be instances where a particular student attempts to take your attention away from class , by taking up the majority of your time in discussion. If this happens, you should take your student's remarks and email the message to the class, asking for additional opinions from other students. Do not let anyone become your favourite student, as when that happens, kids aren't going to wish to hear from your opinions, believing that you only focus on certain students. As a teaching assistant , you must take the time to study the most effective methods from teachers around you. Their expertise and knowledge are available for you to learn from and profit from.

If you meet students who ask questions that aren't connected to the material being taught Explain to the student that as the question isn't related to the material being taught and you'll save it to a later time and will be more than content to respond to his query in the future, but not now. There are students who aren't satisfied with what they are being taught! They always want an increase in their learning, so when this occurs, don't lose temper. Just gently remind that they should be patient since you've planned it out and you want your lessons to be unique!

Students who have been bullies and exhibit disruptive behaviour. When you meet one of them, let them know what you would expect from them. If you enter the classroom, make it explicit what types of conduct which aren't acceptable and the consequences they could face in the event of disobeying. Learn to define your boundaries. You must be assertive, but you must remain at peace. Be aware that you will become their role in their lives!

Thanks and best of luck!

www.ingramcontent.com/pod-product-compliance
Lightning Source LLC
Chambersburg PA
CBHW050400120526
44590CB00015B/1769